Maggie,

With such a ... companion ... your ... just got to enjoy your visit to York.

Bon Voyage

Love Peter.

1981

YESTERDAY WHEN I WAS YOUNG

YESTERDAY WHEN I WAS YOUNG

Charles Aznavour

W. H. ALLEN · London
A Howard & Wyndham Company
1979

Printed and bound in Great Britain at
the Pitman Press, Bath
for the Publishers W. H. Allen & Co. Ltd.,
44 Hill Street, London W1X 8LB

ISBN 0 491 02446 0

Illustrations

Singing with Tom Jones
Singing with Liza Minnelli during his American TV special
Charles—'the man who has everything'—with Ryan O'Neal
while making the film *The Games,* 1969
The Games
Charles, Hardy Kruger and Lino Ventura in *Un Taxi Pour Tobruk*, 1961
Charles and James Coburn filming *The Sky Riders*
Charles and Frank Sinatra in Las Vegas
In St Tropez with Virna Lisi during the filming of *Le Temps des Loups*
Charles and Maurice Chevalier crowning each other
Charles, Bruno Coquatrix and Liza Minnelli in Paris, December 1978
Charles with his children Katia and Misha and their dog
Charles with his son Nicholas
With his wife, Ulla
With Ursula Andress
With Raquel Welch during her only French TV show, *Aznavour Special*
Charles singing in the open air arena in Verona to an audience of 30,000
Charles with his favourite writing partner and brother-in-law, George Garvarentz
Charles, shaking hands with HRH Queen Elizabeth at a Royal Command Performance, 1975

Chapter One

Of course, everyone owes his existence to his parents, but in my case I must add an Italian sea captain without whose intervention it seems I would never have existed, and there would have been no Charles Aznavour.

But I'll begin with my parents. My mother was the eldest daughter of a well-to-do family who could afford to give her a good education. She spoke three languages, and wrote poetry and articles in Armenian. She was born in Turkey, that is in Turkish Armenia which is now nothing but the violated, tombless cemetery of her entire family. Knar Baghdassarian was her maiden name, and she came from a village called Adabazar near Ismit, where her father was a tobacco expert.

My mother had two brothers and one sister, and her mother had married at the age of fifteen which was the usual age for an Armenian girl to marry at the time. My mother was born soon after the marriage.

One day when the family were all in Constantinople (I should say Istanbul), they were all chased from their home, all their possessions were taken from them, and they were forced to take the road of exile from which there was no return for them and a million and half other Armenians. That ought to be the subject of another book, namely the tragedy of the Armenians, but it is not for me to write. I have neither the strength nor the courage to tell their story which I learnt through the tears of my mother and a few relations.

My father's name was Mamigon Aznavourian—Misha to his friends. He was born within the Russian Empire, in a village called Akhaltzikh near Tiflis in Georgia. Monsignor Aghajanian, great prelate of the Vatican, and Mikoyan, the great Soviet statesman were also born in the same village. They all went to the same school, one to become a prelate, one a statesman, and the third an artiste. Isn't it strange that those three boys all made careers addressing audiences, and played their part on the stage of life?

My father was handsome, and appealed to the ladies, especially when he sang. He was a very good singer. He had immense human warmth, making friends wherever he went. He loved giving, and spending money on others, and never counted the pennies. His father was cook in an officers' mess in Imperial Russia, and was furiously opposed to my father embarking on an artiste's career. Poor man, for not only did his son become an artiste, but all his other offspring followed in my father's wake, and are today famous state artistes in Soviet Russia.

When my father left Russia to act and sing abroad, my mother didn't know what to do, being an orphan with only a grandmother to fall back on. So she started to act and sing on the stage. She was outstanding in soubrette-parts in the Molière tradition. Eventually, she appeared in an operetta with my father, and their marriage followed.

Enter the Italian sea captain.

My father had a White Russian passport as he had left Georgia before the Russian Revolution. What I mean is he wasn't a political refugee. When the Turks turned against the unfortunate Armenians again my parents decided to get out of Turkey, their intention to emigrate to the United States. Playing the part of Russian tourists, but with the fear of death in their hearts, they succeeded in reaching an Italian vessel, crowded with refugees whose only crime was that they wanted to remain Armenians and refused to become Moslems.

My mother, who was pregnant, was already on board. My father was just reaching the gangway when a Turkish soldier, who might have overheard a word or two in Armenian as my mother hadn't learned Russian yet, stopped my father. The captain of the ship came to my father's rescue, shouting to the soldier that if he didn't let the passenger embark a diplomatic incident would follow which would cost his officer his career and he, the soldier, would end his life in jail. My father was able to join my mother on the ship.

Their first stop was Salonika in Greece, where my sister was born. She was named Aida because of my parents' admiration for Verdi's opera. My father became secretary to a cousin of my mother's whose local fame lasted till the second world war. His name was Tarah Bey, and he was a fakir by profession. He was also a clairvoyant, a soothsayer and had artistic gifts. People were very impressed by him. Father told us wonderful stories about him. He had studied in India, and knew how to put himself across and play with the credulity of his admirers.

Often the admirers were men of importance such as the chief of the local police who was simple enough to believe that treasure lay hidden, buried in his native village. To lay hands on it, it was absolutely necessary for the fakir to fall into a trance; in fact, several trances. Of course, in order to fall into those trances and meditate while they lasted, the fakir needed money, and naturally, it was provided by the head of the police. The longer the trances lasted the more money had to be provided. Meanwhile a gang of workmen dug up the soil all over the village, making so many holes that the place began to resemble Gruyère cheese. When the chief of police ran out of money and the treasure still wasn't found he realised he was dealing with an impostor, and in his anger he chased the fakir away, which meant that my father lost his job. All that was left for him to do was to continue on his voyage to America with his wife and little daughter.

Their next stop was Marseilles, and from Marseilles they went to Paris, where they hoped to get their visa to the United States. My mother had dreamt of Paris all her young life, but it rained in Paris on the day of their arrival, a great disappointment for her. They went to the American consulate, put their names on the waiting list—and waited. In the eyes of Armenian immigrants America stood for a new, rich life in a land of milk and honey, and for new roots, too, in a vast country where the immigrant could find peace and wealth.

The wait was a long one. My parents went to the consulate every day, and stood among Russians, Greeks and fellow Armenians. Visas were given in sadly small numbers, and one morning they were told that the quota for Armenians was exhausted, and no more visas were available. That was the end of my parents' American dream. Among the Armenians who did receive visas to the States was an actress whose son was to become famous as a film director, Ruben Mamoulian.

My parents weren't unduly depressed. The refusal of the visa was no catastrophe for them, for while they waited for it France had conquered them, and France became their country for the rest of their lives. They felt at home in Paris, and were soon joined by my paternal grandfather, the officers' cook, who had managed to get out of Russia, not to get away from the communists, but to put as big a distance as possible between his wife and a German woman he was in love with and who ran away with him to Paris. He and my father decided to open a restaurant in the town, a restaurant specialising in Russian food. The restaurant opened in the week I was born, at number three rue Champollion.

But first let me speak of my birth.

To begin with the matter of names. First my mother's, whose family name, as I have said, was Baghdassarian, yet on her identity card issued by the Préfecture de Police she figured as Papazian. The error wasn't made by the police but by my father who on the day he went to fetch their identity cards clean forgot her family name when asked for it. So as not to show his ignorance he gave the first name that came to mind, and that name was Papazian.

My mother never forgave him. 'I've lost my parents, brothers and sisters during the massacre of the Armenians,' she said. 'I never heard from or about any of them again. The only thing they left me was my name, and you because of your lack of memory or carelessness took my family away from me for the second time.' This argument, however, didn't seem to interfere with the happiness of their marriage.

Now to my name. Vaghnag was the name of the hero of a novel that had much been read and loved in Armenia. My mother's brother simply adored the novel and the hero, and in memory of him she vowed to name a son Vaghnag if she ever had one. When I was born, on 22 May 1924, the nurse in the Clinique Tarnier in the rue d'Assas, asked my mother what the boy's name would be.

'Vaghnag,' replied my mother.

The nurse just stared at her, probably thinking that she hadn't come round yet. As Vaghnag didn't seem acceptable my mother thought of a venerated uncle whose name was Chalnough. Chalnough might sound better to French ears. And it seemed that it did because when she said Chalnough the nurse's brow cleared.

'You mean Charles,' she smiled.

Thus I became Charles like Charles Trenet and Charles de Gaulle.

As a baby, I understand my parents doted on me, but like most people I can't remember the first years of my life. My sister Aida seems to dominate my early memories, as we quarrelled incessantly. Though she was only a little older than I she looked after me with motherly love, her one obsession being to make me fat, as if a thin brother wasn't worthy of her. I wasn't as thin as all that, as my first photographs show. To get me fat Aida fed me on anything she could lay her hands on. The anything included sweets, bits of meat, coins (though she wasn't rich), buttons, and other unsuitable offerings. I swallowed the lot. Motherly Aida wasn't quite old enough to appreciate the rules of nutrition, and the doctor had often to be fetched post-haste. While my mother sobbed and my cheeks turned from green to red and I was on the verge of suffocating the doctor asked, 'What did he swallow this time?' Aida proudly told him it was either a coin or a button, adding that I liked it very much. On each occasion the doctor tried to explain to her that little children weren't fed on coins or buttons. She didn't agree with him. I was given castor oil or some other unpleasant stuff to make me vomit, and the great fear was over for the time being.

We still lived at the time on the Left Bank, at 24 rue Cardinal Lemoine, and my father's and grandfather's restaurant was at the same address. The restaurant they had at this time was called *Le Caucase*, and whenever they changed restaurants the name remained Caucase (Caucasian). The customers were mostly other immigrants, who paid when they could. People thought father and grandfather were doing well, but what with credit and chalking it up they didn't really prosper.

My father's idea when he opened the first Caucase—there were five in all—was to get together the Russian émigrés, princes and counts, many of them now taxi drivers in Paris. 'They drive their taxis as their servants used to drive their troikas,' observed my father. Not only would they come to the restaurant to have a borscht and drink vodka, but it followed that they would bring their customers too. Seated happily in the restaurant, all the émigrés could weep freely over their past.

To be able to acquire the first Caucase my father and grandfather had to sell the few jewels the family possessed.

When the first Caucase went bust we were living in the rue Saint-Jacques. The restaurant didn't fail for lack of customers. In fact, it was crowded every night. The trouble was that very little money entered the till. There were two reasons for this: the first, father's love of Hungarian gipsy music which lead him to engage eleven gipsy musicians who came specially from Budapest to play in his restaurant. He also engaged two Hungarian dancers at a fabulous fee. He paid their weight in gold. The second reason was credit. At the Caucase practically nobody paid, the customers being mostly students, artists, my parents' numberless friends, and scroungers by the dozen. The whole lot of them signed their bills at the end of the meal, and a fair share of them were never seen again.

One night after the restaurant had closed an old family friend said to my parents, 'If you continue like that you're bound to go bust.'

'Possibly,' said my mother, 'but if we don't help those poor people nobody else will.'

'Some day,' said my father dreamily, 'these young people will all be doctors, engineers, lawyers or generals, and they'll come and pay their bills.'

'God is great and merciful,' said mother. 'He will help us when we are in need.'

My parents belonged to the Church of Armenia, and were true believers.

However, the Almighty didn't consider it the right moment to help the Aznavourian family. In the year of Grace 1930 the *Caucase* had finally to close its door. On the last day while father packed all he could take away, that is take home, two Ethiopian students appeared in the restaurant. They had come to pay their bill.

'It isn't worth while, my children,' said father. 'Keep your money, and have a good time with it.'

The Ethiopians insisted on paying. They were the only two who ever paid, and ever since then father dreamt of travelling to Addis Ababa.

All that remained of the *Caucase* were the kitchen knives. Father had to sell all the rest to pay his debts, and we had to leave the flat and move to cheaper lodgings. Father told us that we had no money left. 'We are poor,' he said to me.

'Does that mean,' I asked, 'that I should go begging in the street?' thinking that in that case I wouldn't have to go to school again.

I was six years old by then.

7

Wherever we moved ours was a strange household, for we were immigrants, and most of our friends were immigrants too. Immigrants are always timorous people, because of their experience of persecution. The Armenians had been persecuted before they came to France, and this did not stop once there. For a start there was the language barrier. My father and a friend of his were knocked about in a Paris street because they were speaking Russian. As a matter of fact, my parents learnt French from Aida and me, though French is only my second language, Armenian being naturally, my mother-tongue.

When I started going to school I managed as an Armenian, to escape the teasing and nastiness of my little schoolmates, because nobody knew anything about the country of my origin. If I said I was an Armenian they just stared at me. It was different with other children of foreign origin. Italians were called dirty macaroni, Jews were called Yids, Negroes were spoken to in pidgin French, and Chinese children were simply laughed at.

All little boys are aggressive by nature and I was no exception, but as nobody attacked me I had no cause to fight. Having no cause, however, wasn't enough to hold me back, so I took the side of the other foreigners, chiefly those who were the most scorned, and fought the boys who ill-treated them. I was always coming home from school with black eyes, cauliflower ears, and torn clothes. And so I became like the other boys, and proud of it too. It gave me a fine sensation of being alive. My parents didn't mind, and in his heart of hearts my immigrant father was proud of this son of his who stood up to the native boys to whom the country belonged. When he saw me with a bleeding nose I think he realised that I had become a native. I looked like the adversaries of Georges Carpentier at the time.

My mother said nothing. She mended my torn clothes, cleaned my wounds and wiped the blood off my nose.

Of my nose I will have plenty more to say.

The Aznavourian family lived in the Latin Quarter, one of the oldest and most interesting neighbourhoods of Paris.

When I stepped out of the haze of early childhood we were living at 36 rue Monsieur le Prince near the Odéon theatre. The proprietors were, I believe, a M and Mme Mathieu who were also the owners of a café nearby. We had a furnished room, four metres by five, with a washbasin but no running water, and an alcove separated from the rest of the room by a grey curtain. A large iron bed took up most of the space in there. We two children slept in a small bed. A wardrobe and a commode and a sofa with broken springs on which slept our great grandmother made up the rest of the furniture. A small iron stove heated the room; and the stove was our kitchen range too. My mother's Singer sewing machine stood in a corner. Most immigrants own such a sewing machine since without it no poor household can exist. Father, mother and her grandmother (the only other member of her family to escape the massacre) Aida and I all had to make do with that room. But that's nothing out of the ordinary. Poor immigrants lived, and probably still live, in such dismal circumstances.

While mother worked on the sewing machine Aida and I were sent out on the landing to play there without disturbing her. The landing smelt of urine as the lavatory of the whole floor was near the sofa covered with imitation leather that was full of holes. Aida and I preferred to go out into the street if the weather was fine enough and breathe fresh air instead of the smell of piss. A flat, round basin, such as one still finds in the Middle East, stood in the middle of our room. This was our bath tub, and armed with a large pitcher, mother would pour water on our small heads, then scrub us properly and wipe us dry. The entire floor was wet afterwards.

We were five human beings in that room, chaste people all of us, and to dress and undress in that space was work worthy of acrobats. The room was sunless and mostly dark, the rue Monsieur le Prince being a narrow street, and the few rooms in the house that received some sunrays were beyond our financial reach. In that semi-darkness mother sewed and mended endlessly.

Among my first memories I can see myself with bread and butter in my hand and probably on my chin too, staring open mouthed at my parents who had turned into frantic creatures, gesturing, declaiming and singing. They were rehearsing dramas, comedies and operettas, and were often joined by other Armenians in love with amateur theatricals. Since they knew but little French they acted in their native language. Their stage performances took place in the Salle des Sociétés Savantes or at the Mutualité or the Salle Iéna. It shouldn't be forgotten that above everything else my parents belonged to the stage. Cooking and sewing were just jobs to keep the family going.

I am often asked when acting and singing entered my life. The answer is even before I was born. I breathed the air of acting and singing from the moment I opened my eyes.

My parents like their Armenian friends acted for the joy of it. They weren't paid, and frequently they rehearsed for a fortnight for only one night's performance. The theatre tickets cost practically nothing, and many members of the audience had free entry to the play or operetta. A number of tickets were sold on credit, and the grateful spectators often forgot to pay their debt. Everybody contributed to the expenses in their own fashion. The dresses were cut and sewn in actors' and spectators' homes, the males made the stage sets, the females prepared the food. Yes, the food. For reasons that are obscure even to me, in eighty per cent of Armenian plays there is a lot of eating on the stage; banquets too at times.

The performance was usually announced for nine o'clock, but the curtain never rose before ten or later because the audience never arrived punctually. The same went for the actors who because of lack of transport—they couldn't afford bus or métro—or working late, couldn't make it in time. Many of them hadn't had a meal before the performance, so they guzzled the food brought for the play before the play began to the indignation of the more conscientious (or better fed) actors! The result was that no food was left for the play. Thus on the stage the actors had to pretend they were eating.

Behind the scenes there was always one person tearing his hair and shouting in despair, and this was the producer, who watched helplessly as the actors changed their lines or forgot them, inventing dialogue or being struck dumb on stage. If it was an operetta the musicians often got the wrong tunes or started too soon or too late. The pianist was generally a Frenchman, that is to say he didn't understand a word of Armenian, so couldn't keep up with the singers. The prompter lost his head on many occasions, and the spectators often heard him before the actors had time to utter the words.

When the curtain fell the women packed the dresses while the men made up the accounts. Usually the play was produced at a loss. Some of the actors, who were specially broke, had kept the price of the tickets they had sold. Much noise and shouting followed, and the exasperated actors (the ones who hadn't kept any money back), rushed to the cloakroom to catch spectators who had acquired their tickets on credit, and try to make them cough up the price.

Frustrated and angry, the actors swore they would never act again, and for forty-eight hours or so there was deep enmity. By then tempers had cooled, and there always was one who went round to see the others, proposing a new play that was sure to break even. Rehearsals started again, and history—their history—repeated itself.

I loved those actors who plied soulless trades all week only to come alive on Sundays on the boards. They acted for the fun of it, for the pleasure of being in communion with the audience, their greatest joy was to rise above their humdrum lives and become kings, princes and other enchanted beings. And I was already one of them, for my acting career had begun at the age of three. Yes, at the age of three.

In 1927 two famous stars came to Paris from Soviet Russia, their name Guierarnian, and they were my aunt and uncle. Naturally, I was taken to the Salle des Sociétés Savantes by my parents. My sister Aida accompanied us. I, who had known only the sort of performances I described above, entered that night for the first time into a real actor's real dressing room. My uncle and aunt took me in their arms, cried with delight in the genuine Armenian fashion, and their stage make-up ran down their cheeks. I was fascinated by it all. The dressing room was incessantly crowded with grandparents, little cousins, long lost friends, young uncles and old nieces. Many tears were dropped, but I remained aloof from all that, watching my uncle busy repairing his make-up after the tears, kisses and embraces. However, by the time my aunt got to her false eyelashes I was thoroughly bored. All that effusion and talk about the past was tedious for a three year old.

I left Aida, who was staring open mouthed at the great man in his flowery dressing gown. She was no taller than the stool on which he sat. I vanished from the dressing room, went into the corridor, saw a staircase, took it, saw a door and went through it. I found myself on the empty stage, but from the other side of the curtain rose a murmur of voices, the murmur as mysterious as the sea. I peeped through the peephole: the auditorium was full. The performance was announced for nine o'clock. Now it was half past nine, but an Armenian audience is capable of waiting for hours to see a play. They love the theatre too much to consult their watches or show any sign of impatience. I for one was too young for the virtue of patience. I recognised in the first row some friends of my parents who came often to see us and to sing with them, accompanied on the *tar*, an Armenian instrument of thirteen cords. I lifted enough of the curtain to let myself through, and I recited the few Armenian poems my mother had taught me. They were about roses and perfumed kisses.

When the great man heard the applause from his dressing room 'What? They dared to start without us,' he roared and the whole family burst on the stage. No, the curtain hadn't risen yet, so no lèse-Guierarnian had taken place, only Aznavourian Junior had declaimed his poems in front of the curtain, and not so badly either as he was loudly applauded. He was lifted by his uncle who took him in his arms, happily explaining, 'God be praised! He isn't like his grandfather. He won't be a cook! He'll be a great artiste!'

When I became famous the Armenians said they weren't astonished, they had expected that ever since that great night. There was room for six hundred in the theatre: today forty thousand say they saw me reciting my poems at the age of three.

I never saw my uncle again. In Russian Armenia there is a theatre called after him, now.

Chapter Two

As a child I was often left to my own devices. I don't mean abandoned in any sense, it was more a respect for my childish liberty. As my parents learnt to speak French from Aida and me they often didn't understand what we said to each other in French. This was just as well because I picked up a lot of swear words playing in the street. I have always been interested—perhaps since that time—in the language of the streets. It is no accident that mine were the first songs in French to use a lot of the vivid words and expressions which are in common use. I shocked quite a few people at the time, including my old idol Maurice Chevalier, who didn't think one should sing words like that. Climates change, and it amuses me to think that I who am not only considered typically French in my manner of singing but who have radically changed the French chanson, have not a single drop of French blood in my veins. Except for the street and school my early life was a strictly Armenian one.

Father used to rise at four or five in the morning, then take a taxi to Les Halles (the market), where he made his daily purchases for the *Caucase*. At home Aida and I played at buying and selling in the Halles. When father came back he went straight to the restaurant. Mother frequently accompanied me to the school, but before school I used to take myself to the nearby church of Saint-Séverin where I acted as altar boy, my Armenian faith notwithstanding. I knew the Catholic Mass by heart, the priests liked me, and I was given a few pennies. I received more at funerals than at weddings. At funerals people weep, so pay no attention to the coins they fork out. It is a different matter at weddings. I mean they are more cautious.

Those were times when people went about their errands without fear, no hold-ups, no attacks in the streets, no bag-snatching, and there were only few motor cars. So I was allowed to come home alone.

In the evenings when the whole family was reunited, father sang, mother told stories, Aida played the piano and sang too. There were always lots of visitors, Armenians, Russians, Jews, Syrians and many other nationalities, and inevitably some Frenchwoman who had fallen in love with the atmosphere of our home. When we lived in the rue Monsieur le Prince, the woman who lived next door became 'Our Frenchwoman'. There was always some excuse for her to be in our house. Either our cat fell out through the window and she brought it back, or her cat fell out and she came to get it. Anyway, she became our faithful friend, loving the picturesque surroundings of the Armenians and their friends. Her name was Mme Tota, and after we left the rue Monsieur le Prince we saw her on and off, and forty years later her son came to spend his holidays with my children in my parents' house in Mougins.

As I have said Aida played the piano well from an early age and I wanted to learn the violin. Father's *Caucase* in the rue Cardinal Lemoine was a refuge and a haven for gypsies and their violins in that age of jazz and Josephine Baker. I would haunt the restaurant and fondle the gypsies' violins. One day I got hold of a violin and I rushed with it into the street, and played. Passersby stopped to gaze fondly at the little violinist. I was only six. A lady was already looking for some coins in her purse when my mother arrived, panting, and deeply ashamed.

'You're mad,' she gasped. 'They will take you for a beggar.'

I looked at her astonished: I had expected to be taken for a fine virtuoso.

Music or song never disturbed our parents as they were singers and musicians themselves, so nobody minded when Aida and I took to writing little songs for ourselves. Slowly I began to learn to play the piano which gave me the right to take part in the family concerts. Everything was an excuse to make music and to sing. Then there was the wireless, and when the wireless was silent we played the gramophone. Despite our eternal financial difficulties father gave us pocket money, 4 francs 75 centimes to be precise. At times of financial stress he hoped that I might be naughty and not deserve the pocket money, but my arguments were always too clever for him. 'He's so reasonable,' he would sigh before putting his hand into his pocket to fork out my 4 francs 75 centimes.

In a café in the place Saint-Michel in the centre of the Latin Quarter there was a gramophone, the forerunner of the juke box, and I spent most of my pocket money listening with earphones to the records it played. One day I received the first big shock of my life—I was nine years old by then—and the shock was a song entitled, *Donnez-moi la main Mamz'elle et ne dites rien* . . . I was so moved and impressed by this song that I decided there and then that I would become a chansonnier. I rushed home to tell Aida about the magic voice I had heard.

'Like Jeanne d'Arc,' she sneered. Well, it was my miracle, and Maurice Chevalier was my archangel.

So much was to happen to me, and circumstances were to push me in different directions now and again, yet subconsciously, that firm decision taken at the age of nine remained my guiding star.

Our parents treated us as equals. Never did they lower their voices when we came into the room to say, 'Look out, the children are here.' When they played cards, we, the children played with them. They stayed up till three o'clock in the morning at times. If they said, 'Children, go and lie down,' we answered, 'We aren't sleepy,' and it was left at that. No scenes: we were our own judges, hence when we felt sleepy we took ourselves to bed without anybody ordering us to. And so it was all along the line.

One extremely hot summer I remember little chums of mine who were made very unhappy. Their parents drank tumblerfuls of water, and they weren't allowed to have any. 'It's bad for your health,' the parents said. 'You'll be bloated if you drink.' The chums just couldn't understand why it was bad for their health but not for their parents'. I drank four glasses of water if I felt thirsty, and I stopped drinking when I felt bloated. I was never punished like so many other children were. There was one exception however.

On the sea of memory a drum comes floating towards me. It was my father's drum, and I hit it and pounded it till it burst. Father loved that drum, so he was furious, and he who hadn't ever beaten me said before he went out, 'This time make him wait up for me. I'll give him the thrashing of his life when I come back tonight.' I, who loved going to bed late, climbed into bed every evening at seven, and pretended to be asleep when father came home. 'Ah, he sleeps,' said father when he arrived. 'Let him sleep now because tomorrow night he'll receive the thrashing.' Then one night he forgot his threat, and the matter wasn't broached again.

Only once did father box my ears. He must have been pretty annoyed since boxing ears wasn't a habit of his. For a whole month I complained of headaches, crying 'Oh! la! la! how my head aches.' And mother exclaimed, 'Misha, you're a monster. You've started beating my children.' It was I who had to stop complaining of headaches because father was suffering far more than I. That, I repeat, was the only time father laid hands on me, and I have followed his example. I never hit my own children.

We were four strikingly different persons, yet we were and remained accomplices and comrades in every manner. None of us had any sense of money. In time I acquired some, probably because my parents had no sense of it.

After I had heard Maurice Chevalier singing *Donnez-moi la main Mamz'elle* I resolved to earn money, not for myself but to help my parents.

Even when things didn't go well the table was always laid for family and friends, and no one ever lacked food in our house. Hors-d'oeuvres, entrées and meat were available at every meal. Father did the shopping which always included a bottle of wine, and when he came back he was invariably pleased with himself, though he had spent his last sou.

'We'll eat well this time too,' he would say at the lunch hour.

'Most certainly,' said mother, 'but what about tonight? Not a franc is left.'

'Children,' said father, 'God is great and He'll provide.'

And provide He did.

My grandfather was a deeply religious man, and grace was said at every meal before we sat down. Our parents were liberal minded, didn't force their faith on us, left us to find our own. I found the same faith as theirs because I had heard father repeat with such conviction that God in His mercy would always help us, and help us He did.

Came the depression of 1930, and we were poorer than ever before. I had to leave school for lack of money. In those days with a school certificate one had a chance of finding a job; today even with the baccalaureat it is far more uncertain. My having to leave school wasn't caused only by the depression; my father had been badly cheated by his partner in the restaurant business. Nothing surprising about that, for the gentleman, who had been treasurer of the Communist Party in Russia, had embezzled the party funds before fleeing to France. It was father's rotten luck to fall on such a partner. However, the Aznavourians weren't rancorous or vengeful people. The embezzler's son came to see us during the war, and was well received.

Poverty or no poverty, depression or no depression, father continued to provide for us with God's help, and also for the many friends who continued coming to the house. Bread plays an important part in poor folk's households. It helps to finish the sauces, takes the place of fingers, and is the background of any meal. It happened one noon that father, who had made his calculations carefully before setting out to buy the food for lunch, clean forgot the item called bread and all money was spent. When mother saw there was no bread he told us not to worry, just get the meal ready, and leave the bread to him. Before he went out he said we should put an extra plate, fork and knife on the table. He returned with a friend he had run into. He had said to him: 'Come and lunch with us, but be so kind and buy some bread first.'

Armenians love good food and good wine which is as much their national drink as the French nation's. When there was a banquet or a feast in our little immigrant world the first thing was to choose a *tamada* who is a sort of toastmaster without whose approval no glass of wine was allowed to be drunk. The guests hadn't even the right to talk without his permission. It isn't words that make the Armenian drink: it is the other way round. The more ideas the *tamada* had the more wine the table companions swallowed. Toasts were drunk, ordered by the *tamada* to those present, not the lot of them, but to each individually. Then one drank to those absent and to the dead. After that other excuses had to be found for more toasts and wine.

As father had a happy nature and was an excellent mixer it was mostly he who acted as *tamada* at the gatherings I attended. Father loved the year 1903 for reasons I don't know. He would start his stories invoking that year. 'Papa,' I would interrupt, 'you were only six at the time.' One night when the guests had drunk to uncles in South America, to actor friends, to the Greek ship that had brought some of them from Istanbul, to the French government for having given them asylum, to the stone bridge and the wooden bridge subjects seemed to have run out. But father couldn't be beaten. He raised his glass to company water, then to gas and then to electricity.

To go back to my leaving school, when we moved to the rue Cardinal Lemoine we found that our flat was opposite a school for actors. It was the École du Spectacle, run by Mme Maréchal and M Rognoni of the Comédie Française.

'That's where you'll study now,' said father.

The hand of fate one could easily say. Fate had brought little Charles to the flat that faced a school for actors. But don't our own inclinations force fate at times?

First I wasn't pleased with the prospect. I would lose my cherished independence by frequenting a school on the other side of the street. Just crossing over and returning the same way, no chance to loiter, trail in the gutter, play with my fellow pupils, and no excuses to arrive back late. However, when it was explained to me that it was a school for future actors my whole attitude changed.

But I did have an earlier experience of the theatrical world—the real one. I was nine years old when I wrote to the Théâtre du Petit-Monde without my parents' knowledge. I received a reply, asking me to go to the theatre for an audition. I showed the letter to my mother who came with me. On that day I met for the first time those loud, stupid creatures, the parents who believe their children will become stars. The worst were those mothers who had failed becoming actresses themselves.

Among those waiting for the audition were little girls made-up in the most blatant manner, little boys in their Sunday best. Some cried, others fought each other, and above the din the mothers shouted the praise of their children's talent. Poor mother stood apart from them as boasting wasn't her line. I wasn't wearing my Sunday suit for the simple reason that I didn't possess one. Mother and I waited side by side in a corner. Whenever the door opened mothers and offspring pushed forward. When there was practically none left except for us two M Humble, the director of the theatre called out, 'Anybody left?'

'Me,' said I in a timid voice.

'What can you do?'

'Dance.'

'Good. Got your score with you?'

I produced an old yellow score which I gave the pianist. I had learnt all on my own a Caucasian dance with plenty of kicking of legs. When I had finished M Humble asked whether I had come alone. I pointed at mother who came up.

'Leave your address,' M Humble said. 'I'll write to you.'

As we left a mother whispered to us, 'When he says that it means he won't engage him.'

Mother and I went home on foot in order to save money. She was sad while I felt humiliated. Two days later a letter arrived, telling us I was engaged.

And in fact I was a Caucasian dancer in the *Un Bon Petit Diable*. I had also another part, wearing a beard. That took place in the old theatre of the Trocadéro at Christmas 1933.

Thus I had some theatrical experience when Aida and I became pupils of the École du Spectacle. My parents didn't send us to that school in the hope of us making a career on the stage: they didn't think of careers. They sent us because it was the nearest school. Perhaps our concierge was impressed by the stage, but none of us was since the stage was in our blood.

Aida and I took our time crossing the street, that is to say we loitered a bit before going into the school. We were the worst dressed pupils. The others always wore their best clothes in fervent expectation of some famous impresario looking in and catching their eye. Or even the manager of a small theatre.

'We chose France because of 1789,' father declared, 'the year liberty came to the French. I don't see why I shouldn't give my son the same liberty.'

In my freedom I dressed as the fancy took me.

In the mornings I rushed round the nearby streets in the company of a little black boy. Before going to school I bought a few sweets with the modest sums mother gave me to which I added my tips as altar boy at Saint-Séverin. I nicknamed my coloured friend Bamboula. It amused me to imitate his accent, and to speak *petit nègre* became an obsession. I spoke with that accent the whole day long which irritated my parents and Aida. Yet that obsession became quite useful when I was engaged as a little Negro in *Emil and the Detectives* in the Studio des Champs-Elysées. I caught the director's attention when to amuse my fellow pupils I acted the *petit nègre* in the school's playground.

The École du Spectacle was fundamentally for children who had already found engagements. If they had an audition or a rehearsal in the morning they were entitled to come in the afternoon, if it was in the afternoon then they had to be in in the morning.

So I was beginning to earn my living. Aida earned hers too, singing and dancing. It was high time too because father's affairs weren't progressing. He had a bistro at the time, and it wasn't for lack of customers that it didn't prosper. The reasons for its decline were the same as the earlier *Caucases:* too easy credit and no money coming in. One night at dinner father declared that the bistro was sold and we were moving.

We moved to the impasse de Béarn in the middle of the Jewish quarter of Paris. The ceilings were low, the wall paper olive green, a dark apartment in every sense. All my new friends were Jewish boys of my age. A new music entered my ears, a music close to Russian and Armenian music. Their food was also similar to ours.

Aida and I continued going to the École du Spectacle, but with less and less enthusiasm. She had already got a contract with M Prior who was a singer and a music editor in the Fauborg Saint-Martin. I didn't lag behind. I played the part of the small Henri IV in *Margot*, Edouard Bourdet's play, at the Théâtre de Marigny in which I had to speak with a Béarnais accent. Then I was a choir boy, the part silent, in *Much Ado About Nothing*. Then helped by Aida I learnt a few songs, and applied to the Petit Casino, but was refused because I was too young.

We often played truant while we were still at the École du Spectacle. We went to the cinema instead of studying at the school. We went to early performances that started at ten in the morning. Our favourites were musicals, Fred Astaire and Ginger Rogers our heroes.

One day Aida suggested taking me to M Prior who at the time had a troupe of child actors. A boy had left the troupe, so there might be a chance for me. I jumped at it, and we went to see M Prior and his wife Mina who ran the troupe with him, and his first question was whether I could imitate a Marseilles accent. I could imitate any accent, so I was engaged. We rushed home with the happy tidings.

'Who's Prior?' mother asked father.

'A good popular singer,' said father. 'He sells five hundred records of each of his new songs.'

That impressed mother.

'I'll earn fifty francs a month, and will be fed, lodged and dressed,' I said.

That was even more impressive.

M Prior's troupe was like a big, happy family. The older children looked after the younger, and Mme Prior was manageress and nanny at the same time. I felt contented among them. Besides, I earned more than fifty francs a month. As M Prior was a music editor too he had to send scores to different conductors all over France. I attended to the dispatching of the scores for which I was paid separately. I also imitated Charlie Chaplin very well.

When we went on tour we travelled in a little old bus the Priors had acquired. Mme Prior didn't care for fast driving, M Prior hated backseat drivers.

'You drive too fast,' she would say.

'But, Mina, it's only forty kilometres an hour.'

'Much too fast. You'll kill the lot of us.'

'Mina, leave me in peace.'

So it went every time we got into the little old bus.

On the stage we were dressed in white with a red flannel belt. The first part of the performance were the children, the second M Prior with his Marseillais songs. I remember Bruno, the conductor and accordion player, Palmyre, his sister, who played the xylophone, Toni Ovia who played the guitar and sang like Tino Rossi, and of course Aida who sang, danced and played the piano. I did imitations and played the métalophone and the bells. The star of the troupe and the apple of M Prior's eye was Harry Scanlon who sang in the Maurice Chevalier manner. In the second part of the performance we children played the instruments, that is were the orchestra that accompanied M Prior while he sang.

We went on tour for eight months a year, visiting most of France and Belgium. There was no going on tour in summer. The Priors rented a house in the Basses-Alpes, where they kept us the whole hot season. In fact, we holidayed with them. It was a grand life, my only sorrow that I wasn't allowed to imitate my idol, I mean Maurice Chevalier, as that was Harry Scanlon's job. I often wished he would fall sick, but he had an iron constitution.

Then one sad day it all came to an end. The Priors had to disband the troupe because it had cost them too much. When we said goodbye to them with tears in our eyes it was like leaving part of our family.

I had far more confidence now, thanks to my time with the troupe. That confidence was badly needed because father wasn't prospering at all. I was earning up to six hundred francs a month which came in handy at home. But, alas, I was growing out of my child actor's boots. I was too old to play a child, too young to be given adult parts. So the time came when I found myself without a job. Still, the confidence was there.

I had memorised a number of chansons while I was with the Priors, and this turned out to be enormously helpful. I succeeded in having an audition in Henri Varna's presence at the Alcazar, and because of the Marseillais accent I had learnt I was given a part in *Vive Marseilles!* which lasted for three months. After that Aida and I sang in the Bar des Vedettes at Radio 37, and then I was offered a *crochet* at the Globe, the big café on the boulevard de Strasbourg. A *crochet* is a singing competition with cash prizes. It is called a *crochet* because if a competitor sings too badly a huge hook appears on the stage which lifts him off it. I never had to make the acquaintance of the *crochet*.

I was delighted when the idea was put to me. The first time I competed was in a brasserie at the Palais Berlitz. The trouble was that you had to consume a drink or a coffee before putting down your name, and our finances were pretty shaky. Father ordered a coffee, and I, making myself even smaller than I was, vanished into a corner so as not to be noticed by the waiter. The first prize was fifty francs, the second thirty, the third ten. Though competitors were legion father and I had already made plans in case I got one of the prizes. If it was the fifty francs, we could redeem the samovar we had had to hock the other day. I waited for my turn with three songs, one of them, naturally, *Donnez-moi la main Mamz'elle*. Certainly that was the song that influenced me most to become a singer, not so much the song itself but the manner in which Maurice Chevalier sang it.

Well, I won the first prize every time I competed. There was one exception, namely at the Globe, where I only got the second prize. The first went to a man with a powerful voice who had sung *Le Rêve Passe*, in which a little boy dreams about Napoleon and sees his hussars, dragoons and the Guard.

On our way home I said to father, 'You see, Papa, the French love powerful voices, and my voice isn't a strong one.'

That was something I worried about for a long time.

Chapter Three

I went on hearing 'you're too big' or 'you're too small' whenever I applied for an engagement. It was a sort of twilight, no longer the day and not yet the night with its stars. Gone were the days when the manager of the Petit-Monde beamed on his small Caucasian dancer.

A tiny part now and then, perhaps as a film extra was all that came my way. 'I want to become an actor, and learn to dance and sing,' I used to whine when I came home in the evenings.

'As you can't earn your living with your feet any more,' said father, 'you'll have to do something with your hands.'

Armenians respect people who know how to use their hands. Using your hands you can become a tailor or a cobbler. Father had said that after he had approached a rich Armenian to help me to make a theatrical career.

'A theatrical career?' spluttered the rich Armenian. 'An actor? An artiste? You're mad. Our race is made for manual work or commerce. I'm willing to help your son if he's ready to learn a trade. But if you continue dreaming of the stage you won't get a sou out of me.'

My parents gave in, and I had no other choice than to give in too. My parents were convinced that learning a trade could do me no harm. With the rich Armenian's help I became a pupil at the Central School of Radio in the rue de la Lune. I worked diligently and was bored stiff.

Aida came to my rescue. She was studying with Jean Tissier at the Théâtre des Variétés, and as she could imitate our parents' handwriting she wrote letters of excuses to the school authorities to enable me to accompany her to the theatre from time to time. I was fascinated by Jean Tissier with his professional nonchalance. He taught his pupils to use their shortcomings to their advantage.

'Believe me, my little ones,' he would say, 'shortcomings are part and parcel of an actor's personality.' He gave us the great Jouvet as an example. Jouvet stammered yet was a giant, whereas another actor (whose name he gave us but meant nothing to us) whose elocution was perfect was only a pygmy. He gave me little parts such as the Viceroy of Péru in Prosper Mérimée's play *Carosse du Saint-Sacrament*, a bit humiliating to be only a viceroy to one who had acted the child Henri IV.

But all that didn't interfere too much with my studies at the Central School. Sadly I asked myself who would come to my rescue to lift me out of my humdrum existence.

It was the Germans.

War had been declared, and the face of Paris changed immediately. People became different, their joie de vivre evaporated, and there were long queues in front of food shops. I overheard a housewife observing that the food restrictions were odious because the unfortunate children would suffer in their growth. If, I thought, anybody comments on my short figure later on I will say that it was the fault of the war rather than having a short mother. In easier times I would have been taller.

For the Aznavourians the war meant that we would have to continue with our dear unorganised life despite the food tickets, the power cuts and the curfew—but with a difference.

Shortly after the outbreak of war father came home in the evening with a curious expression, partly proud, partly grave.

'What's wrong?' mother asked.

'I joined up,' said father.

Tears ran down all cheeks, including father's.

'But why did you do that?' asked Aida.

'Nobody asked you to,' said mother.

'That's quite true,' said father, 'but this country has been generous to us, and gave us the chance to survive. At such moments we must show our gratitude. Besides, I'd be ashamed to walk round the streets the healthy man I am while all other able-bodied men were at the front.'

Then in loud Armenian he declared how he regretted not having been able to fight in every war of France since 1789.

One autumn afternoon the call-up papers arrived. Father packed his suitcase, and with the packed suitcase and his *tar* he left for the Gare d'Austerlitz. Nothing and nobody should separate him from his beloved musical instrument. Naturally, the whole family accompanied him to the station. Generally the called-up men left by the Gare du Nord or the Gare de l'Est, but father's training camp was down south near the Pyrenees. As I watched the train pull out then disappear I, who was born in France and considered myself a Frenchman, realised once again what it meant to be an immigrant.

Father wasn't unhappy in the training camp, so his reassuring letters said. The camp was for foreign volunteers, and there were thousands of Jews, Russians, Roumanians, Greeks and Armenians. Father soon became an army cook, and his cooking pleased the volunteers. In the evenings he played the *tar*.

Father's departure changed everything for me. I, who had been interested only in the theatre and songs, had to lay my ambitions aside, for I knew it was up to me to provide for the family. I must be the breadwinner. The last *Caucase* had been sold to pay for what we owed, so no outside help could be counted on. Mother worked as seamstress in a large shop in the afternoons, but her earnings weren't enough to make both ends meet. That decided me to earn my living as a news vendor. Though my voice wasn't strong—remember the man who bellowed *Le Rêve Passe* and got the first prize at the *crochet*—as a news vendor it was as loud as a car-horn.

My itinerary was invariably the same: I set out from the rue du Croissant, then came the Bourse, then the Champs-Elysées after selling my papers at the Opéra and the Madeleine. I had to sell them on the move as I hadn't a permit or owned a kiosk. Usually I sold every paper, and when they were sold I returned to the rue du Croissant to get a new batch. If I was lucky and saw a lorry going in that direction I hung on to it. It was a heavy, tiring task, but I did make a living, helped the family, and while I sold the papers I had ample leisure to dream of the theatre and actors. And one day at the corner of the avenue George V and the Champs Elysées I recognised a singer whose voice I liked, I also possessed some of his records. I stopped in front of him, and held out a newspaper and a slip of paper. He took the newspaper, put his autograph on the slip of paper, then put his hand into his pocket to take out a coin.

'No,' I said, 'I am giving you the paper.'

'Why?'

'Because I want to.'

'Well, I want to pay for it, and as I'm the elder of the two you must accept it.'

Newspapers then cost twenty-five centimes. He gave me fifty, telling me to keep the change.

The singer was Ray Ventura, and meeting him was the greatest pleasure that came my way in my news vendor's career.

'We will win because we are the stronger,' shrieked the huge posters on the walls of Paris during the phoney war. People believed them, and nobody seemed worried. Everybody expected Hitler to attack the Maginot Line and thus lose the war, and swiftly at that. So much has been written about the fall of France that I don't think it is necessary here to talk of the Parisians' reactions as the Germans fast approached the Town of Light, which in any case was pretty dark owing to the black out. With the great exodus when most of the population left Paris my job as news vendor came to an abrupt end. So I was out of work, and soon we wouldn't have the means of survival.

The last we heard from father was that his regiment was leaving the training camp. He warned us not to follow those who were running from Paris, but to stay put. So the question of us leaving didn't arise.

'The Germans,' said a neighbour to mother, 'are mad about scent, stockings and chocolate, the dirty swine.'

I nodded to myself when I heard those words. I had a little money put aside, and went to buy chocolate bars with it, not the big ones, but the small bars. It wasn't expensive. I kept them in my room—waiting.

Many people who intended to decamp left their bicycles at the stations before forcing their way into the overcrowded trains. Some chums of mine suggested we go to the stations to see what could be done with those deserted bikes. They lay around in heaps and piles, and we brought back about forty which we left in the garage of a friend. You never knew.

Another chum asked me to go into partnership with him to buy bottles of scent. 'The more they stink the more they want them,' he said. We bought as much scent as we could afford. It was sure to come in useful.

I saw the Germans entering Paris as I stood outside the métro station of the rue de Cadet, and was as surprised as the rest of the remaining Parisians. We had been told on the radio and in the papers that they were a ragged, starving army, and lo! we beheld handsome rosy cheeked giants full of health, well fed and smiling.

'Merde,' said an astonished man, standing next to me.

A German motorbike with a sidecar stopped beside us. The two soldiers gave us sweets and cigarettes. Though radio and newspapers had incessantly warned us that the Germans distributed poisoned sweets I accepted them the same way as the other people near me. Then appeared a lorry from which the soldiers, as if to prove they possessed butter as well as guns, threw us butter and oil. I took all I could lay my hands on and carry away.

'They buy anything you offer them,' said my chums when I got back to our street. 'You can ask any price you want. They're too stupid to argue.'

I listened carefully to all they said. I would sell the Germans anything I could get hold of. I would become a black marketeer and keep the family alive. Not bad to be a black marketeer at the age of sixteen, I proudly thought. Proud is the word. In a rich country like France earning one's living so young doesn't mean much, but we Aznavourians came from a poor background, and I was as proud of earning my livelihood as are even today children in South America, in the East and in Africa. All I earned I took back home.

On that day of the Germans' entry into Paris my pals and I sallied forth with the goods we had collected before they came, but took only small quantities at a time lest we made ourselves conspicuous. I took myself to one of the city gates, where German troops came past in lorries, one behind the other. Suddenly a column of lorries stopped. I approached one a little apprehensively. In a timid voice I said, 'Chocolate?' Eyes lit up and hands came forward.

'How much?' they asked in German.

'One mark for three bars,' I said, now really afraid since they hadn't cost me more than five francs, and the value of the occupation mark was twenty francs. In less than ten minutes I had sold the lot. Then I cycled home to get more.

Within a week my stock of chocolate was gone, and there was no chance of buying more. I fell back on the scent, but that went quickly too.

Now only the bicycles were left. However, they had to be repaired first. Despite our not having paid for the cycles the profit was small owing to the money the repairs cost us. There was no new stock of cycles forthcoming either as nobody left them unattended any more. In short, the great, opulent days were over.

Father reappeared, saying, 'We're all together again, praised be God.'

He had had plenty of adventures, hurrying in the daytime, sleeping in lofts at night, and picking fruit when hungry. Now and then a peasant felt sorry for him, and gave him a bowl of soup. He was given civilian clothing, and was thus able to return on foot to Paris.

Mother told him how well I had looked after the family in his absence. He was pleased. Then he asked at what time the curfew began. Mother said, 'In two hours time.'

'So I've got time to see friends,' he said, changed, went out, and when he came back he announced that he had found work as headwaiter in an Armenian restaurant.

So we were able to carry on without chocolates, scent and cycles.

I met my first professional black marketeers in a café on the Champs-Elysées. Leaning against the counter one of them asked those present whether they knew anybody interested in buying a lorry load of sugar. Another suggested bartering a kilo of coffee against two bicycle tyres. The lorry load of sugar was above my means, but tyres were up my street, for at the time we lived above a garage in the rue Lafayette. There were no employees in the garage for the simple reason that no cars were left in it. If anybody came to the garage in the hope of finding a mechanic to repair his car—only few were allowed to use cars—I jumped to it, and did the repairs.

In time we parted company from the garage. We had to move because the house was on the verge of collapsing. We found a flat in the rue de Navarin, three proper rooms and a kitchen, all a bit dark but without the fear of the roof coming down on us. The big advantage was the cellar, for Armenians do need cellars to store the superfluous stuff they never use yet drag with them.

While I sold, bartered and repaired the occasional car I never forgot my vocation. It burned within me, my one true flame. With father earning his living again I could try finding an engagement—any engagement—again. After an audition I was engaged by the Jockey, a nightclub and cabaret up in Montparnasse. I rushed straightaway to the Kommandantur on the Place de l'Opéra to get an *Ausweiss* to authorise me to stay out after the curfew.

On the first evening the Jockey's manager nearly collapsed when I arrived. All I possessed as garments at that time were a claret-coloured sweater and a pair of brown trousers. I told him I had nothing else to put on, and in any case trousers and sweater were preferable to singing naked. Besides, the spectators would consider it rather avant-garde.

Like most Parisians I had become accustomed to the drab life under the German boot. Nevertheless, I could realise one of my childhood dreams while I worked at the Jockey, namely going home at two in the morning on roller-skates. I was a roller-skate maniac, thus the long journey from Montparnasse to the rue de Navarin was more fun than drudgery.

On the first night as I sailed home on my roller-skates I was stopped by a German patrol in the rue des Pyramides. They stared and glared simultaneously at me, nothing astonishing about that as I still wore my stage make-up and carried a score under my arm. They asked what I was doing. I said I worked in a nightclub, and showed my *Ausweiss*. They examined it for a long time before they let me go. That scene repeated itself every night. I came to know almost every German patrol in Paris. The only night I didn't have the *Ausweiss* on me—I had forgotten to renew it—not one patrol stopped me although I saw several on my way home.

I heard from an acquaintance that actors were being engaged for a revue that would go on tour. The address was 18 rue Pigalle. I went, and was asked by a M James what I could do. I said I sang, danced and acted. He sent me to see Jean Cazenave whom I knew well. At the age of nine I was taken to Metz with a children's troupe for a gala performance. Cazenave was one of the troupe. Mother had given me a thermos flask full of hot tea. I dropped and broke it on the station platform. 'Don't worry,' said the kind Cazenave, 'I've got one and we'll share it.' Then he broke his too.

I was engaged, so I left the Jockey. In a troupe I was nearer to what I wanted from life. I signed the contract for little money indeed though the work was hard. The day will come, I said to myself, when I will dictate the terms. However, in the meantime I must grab anything that comes my way.

I think that my determination to succeed and get to the top was caused by the humiliations and underpayments of my youth.

I had quite a lot to do in the revue. I began with my repertoire of songs, then came an apache dance, then an acrobatic dance with the star of the troupe, Sandra Dolza, and then I followed with some comic sketches. Finally, some *tableaux vivants*, so I was pretty busy. The great moment for the public was when the female dancer in the last scene came slowly to the edge of the stage to let the eyes get accustomed to her, and when they had she turned her back on them, showing her naked buttocks for exactly three seconds. The things one had to do to earn one's living!

The day of our departure arrived at last. Our first stop would be the town of Sedan. When my suitcase was packed mother filled a glass of water, an old Armenian custom when one goes on a long journey. As I came out of the house I saw mother at the window, holding the glass of water. As I went past the window she threw the water behind me. You go like water, you will come back like water.

The troupe climbed into a train, the coaches were old, the engine suffered from asthma, and it slowed down when it approached a bridge (I will have more to say about trains slowing down before bridges), stopped at every station and often in the bleak countryside for long hours.

Jean Cazenave and I became bosom friends during the tour. He also taught me the rudiments of seduction. One night after the performance in Sedan I found myself with him in the company of two sisters who belonged to the troupe. We were in a dark street, and for the life of me I can't remember how that meeting came about. I was timid, and didn't know what to say, afraid too that some stupid observation I might make would spoil everything.

'How will we arrange it?' said Jean suddenly, going straight to the point.

We were all staying in a dismal, wretched hotel. Jean and I had to share the same bed, and so did the sisters whose room was as small as ours. There was but one answer to the dilemma.

I hate the cold, and it was terribly cold in Sedan that night.

As we stood there shivering I suddenly took the hand of the taller sister. A big girl like that would surely warm me in bed. Astonished by my temerity Cazenave took the other sister's hand, then the four of us went back to the hotel. I took my key, he took the girl's key, I took my girl, whose name was Christiane, to my room and bed, and Cazenave took the sister to theirs. I didn't shiver with cold that night.

Christiane and I were a happy couple. Every day we put a little money aside which we sent to our respective families. We were good, decent children of our parents despite our living in sin.

Though I am short my nose is long. It hasn't stayed so long, but the story of my nose will come later in the book. In Sedan it was still conspicuously long. One morning there was a loud knock on the door: a German soldier from the Kommandantur.

'It's about your nose,' said Christiane.

I knew what that meant. I followed the German soldier to the Kommandantur, not for the first time, and once again I was in the presence of the German charged with Jewish affairs.

'Where were you born?' he asked.

'In Paris.'

'Your parents?'

'In Armenia.'

'Are you a Jew?' His eyes were focused on my nose.

'Not in the slightest.'

'What's your religion?'

'Gregorian-Armenian.'

'Have you any proof?'

I showed him my certificate of baptism in the Armenian

35

church in Paris which mother had sent me in order to be on the safe side. Because of my nose the Germans continued suspecting me, and questioned the other members of the troupe about me.

It was getting colder and colder in Sedan. The hotel wasn't heated, and the cold is no inspiration for a seducer. I used to get into bed at night wearing my sweater, and would wake in the morning clinging to Christiane's big body. My only real relaxation was the public baths, where you weren't allowed, however, to stay more than half an hour.

One night after the performance Cazenave came to tell me he was leaving the troupe. I asked whether he had something better in view. It wasn't that: he was tired and fed up with working so hard for so little money. He added he didn't care whether he found a new job or died of starvation as long as he died in his own comfortable bed at home.

'This is most annoying,' I said. 'Who'll play the piano if you go?'

'None of my business. I'm off to Paris tomorrow morning at eight o'clock.'

And he kept his word.

Our orchestra was in a disastrous state, consisting only of a trumpet and a drum. Cazenave wasn't the first to leave. In the afternoon our manager asked me whether I could play the piano.

'With one finger only.'

'Perfect,' he said. 'You'll take M Cazenave's place at the piano.'

I observed I couldn't do all the work he wanted from me without him paying me more. The man was a tight-fisted Auvergnat, and it took me a long time to force him into giving me a rise. I was beginning to learn that if they need you they give in, if they don't they fling you out. I asked for fifty francs more: we settled for twenty-five, not too bad in the circumstances.

'You're jolly clever to have got such a sum out of an Auvergnat,' said Christiane admiringly.

That same night I started on my new job. It was too much of a good thing in that I had to jump into the orchestra pit after my apache dance to play the piano, then back on the stage for my acrobatic dance, then down into the pit again to accompany the naked dancers. While I played I had to change, so played with the left hand only during the time my right hand was busy with the clothes, then with the right hand to let the left hand take its share. It was worthy of a contortionist. After a few days I was sick and tired of it.

We left Sedan and the cold weather.

My parents and I were always a mutual aid society. Now that I needed a new set of clothes for the furtherance of my stage career they sold all their furniture without a murmur, that is the fake Louis XIII furniture in the dining room, the bed and wardrobe in their bedroom, and they slept on mattresses. It didn't worry them since sooner or later money would come in with God's help again, and then new furniture could be bought. And what did furniture matter if the artiste son had to go on tour!

I fitted myself out with that money. Bought a white jacket, a dinner jacket, in short everything I needed for the tour.

Orléans was the troupe's next stop, and there catastrophe awaited me. As we got out of the train I asked my companions whether they had seen my big trunk which contained my parents' furniture so to speak. Nobody had seen it. Like one demented I looked into every carriage, and rushed along the platform with tears in my eyes. The trunk had vanished. I raced to the police though I was certain that wouldn't help, but on the other hand it kept me busy during the first awful minutes that followed my loss.

So everything was gone. My parents were left without their furniture, I with only the suit I wore. I wouldn't have another suit for two endless years.

My heart was no longer in it, and Christiane tired me. The answer was to see the manager, and ask for a new rise.

'This time you're going too far,' shouted the manager.

I chucked my job, took leave of Christiane, and returned to Paris in my only suit.

'We are together again the four of us,' said father happily.

Chapter Four

Perhaps it is no accident that I have always regarded a sense of humour and an ability to show emotion as the most important things in life. In my family we laughed together and we cried together easily and often. Those characteristics, as well as my parents' unusual love of the stage, were to prove my greatest blessings.

Through my sister Aida I met Jean-Louis Marquet. Neither of us could have imagined that he would become my impresario. He was at the time of our meeting the director of the Club de la Chanson, where the members were all authors and composers. Marquet's act consisted of telling stories as he couldn't sing to save his life.

I asked him and Aida how they had run into each other. He and friends had gone to see her at the Concert Mayol. The Concert Mayol was an institution in Paris, the poor man's Folies Bergères, one could say. On the stage there invariably appeared girls dressed in black evening dresses up to the neck. When they turned their back on the audience the spectators' eyes lit up at the sight of their naked buttocks. Aida didn't perform among them as her part was very chaste. In the middle of all that flesh a singer would come on the stage, usually a young beginner as the Concert Mayol couldn't afford to pay high fees. There were daily auditions to find a young man or woman who could hold the stage for fiteen minutes. Some of the great stars began their career at the Concert Mayol. People like Yvette Guilbert, Maurice Chevalier and Fernandel.

To return to the Club de la Chanson. I went there that night with Aida to see what it was like. The first person I ran into was Pierre Roche whom I had already met at the École du Music Hall. As you will see, he became my partner for many years, but neither of us had any inkling of that when I went to the Club for the first time.

Pierre was the scion of a noble family and had dropped the *de* when he embarked on his stage career. Although still young he was losing his hair. He wore a signet ring with the family crest on it, and he was the president of the Club.

As it was early when we arrived only a few people were around. Pierre sat down at the piano, and accompanied Lawrence Riesner who sang a chanson. Marquet joined Aida and me to explain the aim of the club, namely, promoting singers, dancers and writers of sketches and lyrics. They were moving to the rue Ponthieu, where they had found larger premises. All the performers were accompanied on the piano by Pierre Roche. I asked whether I could be of any use to them. The answer was that I would deal with the publicity side. Tickled, I accepted, and joined the club.

On the opening night in the rue Ponthieu there were about four hundred guests. Among them was Edith Piaf. Food and champagne were served, and in those days of restrictions they were the real centre of attraction. We, the naive members of the Club were proud of the success of the opening night. Many of the guests, who had left replete and heavy with drink, never came near the Club again.

In spite of it all it worked. Lectures and lessons in the day time, cabaret in the evening, and jazz sessions at night. The audiences were a mixed lot—Resistance workers, deserters, Jews, black marketeers, and even collaborators. We, the performers, usually stayed the entire night on the premises as only a few of us possessed an Ausweiss. Into that mixed assembly the Gestapo burst one night. It was sheer panic, but luckily the Gestapo didn't know of the existence of the emergency door through which most people managed to escape. Also, somebody had cut off the electric light, and that helped too. I escaped through a skylight, remaining on the roof till the Gestapo left. Their only catch was Lawrence Riesner who had an American mother. He was questioned the whole night, and released only in the morning.

The trouble with the Club de la Chanson was that it didn't bring in any money. Father being out of work, our situation was really bad, so something had to be done about it. Father, who always found a solution, applied for a permit to sell goods in the market places of the Department of Seine-et-Oise. It was granted, and we cycled to the different markets to sell socks and stockings. We didn't do too well with them. We changed over to sausages, with which we did much better. Enghien was one of the towns we visited. I sang there on café terraces accompanied by an accordion. I bought a new bicycle with the money my singing brought in.

Now and then I went with father as far as Yvetot to bring butter, eggs, cheese and poultry back to Paris. At the station in Paris the control was severe. (Officially you were only allowed to buy food with food tickets.) A customs man stopped me one day to ask, 'What have you got in your bulging pockets?'

'They're full of butter,' I answered, looking him in the eye.

'Get on with you. Hop it, I don't like jokes,' he said.

I had five kilos of butter in my pockets.

We ate part of the food we brought back from those expeditions; the rest we sold.

It is difficult for those who haven't lived through the Occupation and all the misery it brought to understand the struggle for survival of my generation. Today everything can be got easily: we dreamed of ham and cakes, as children nowadays dream of winning the Tour de France or owning a private space ship.

I was down to my last pair of shoes, decrepit shoes which the cobbler couldn't repair any more.

Despite my journeys with father I continued to go to the Club de la Chanson. I suggested to Pierre Roche that we should give lessons in singing at the Club. Roche had an indolent nature, and he loved sleeping late. Two hours would be plenty, he said after I had succeeded in persuading him that even two hours every day would add up to years in the long run. We shook hands on it, and thus our long partnership started. Our first pupils were the Fontaine sisters, one of whom later married Francis Blanche.

We arranged their repertoire of songs, along with a lot of gesturing which we considered necessary. Roche and I were continuously at the Club, I looking for pupils, he for a girl to take home.

Most things seem to come about by mistake. Roche and I appeared in a gala performance at Beaumont in the Oise. By then I had ceased to be Aznavourian in the profession. People considered the name too long, so it was shortened to Aznavour, and Aznavour it remained. At the Concert Mayol Aida was billed as Aida *Aznamour* which was the big idea of the Concert Mayol's director. On the programme Roche came first, and in fact was the star. I came fifth, so there would be three numbers between us. The announcer was Lyne Jack of the Concert Mayol, and she had been so accustomed to seeing us together that she announced Charles Aznavour and Pierre Roche to the audience as if we sang together. Of course, she should have announced Pierre Roche only.

Roche and I stared at each other. Then he said, 'Let's go. It might be quite funny.'

We appeared on the stage, and we sang the three chansons we had taught the Fontaine sisters. Our triumph was enormous. We were called back again and again, and as we knew no other songs we repeated them to the audience's delight.

We were congratulated by all our friends. Marquet offered to act as our impresario, assuring us that he would get good contracts. 'In no time you'll be stars the pair of you.'

Truly enough he got us an engagement in Lille. When we got there I discovered to my utter fury that we were billed as

The Two of the Rhythm. 'This is breaking the contract,' I shouted, but Roche just smiled, lying as usual on the hotel bed. It was too much effort to lose his temper. Ten pretty ballet dancers were in the performance too, and that was sufficient to keep him quiet.

I love women, and women have played enormously important parts in my life. However, with Roche love was a daily preoccupation, which came before anything or anybody else. He was insatiable. A day without a girl was a lost day for him. Tall and slim, with the manners of a nobleman, the patience of a crocodile and the pomposity of a bishop, he often won where the handsomest young men had lost the battle.

It was, as will be seen, partly Roche's doing, that is to say, his doing nothing except fornicating, that made me start writing lyrics. I am not a person who can stay in bed all the time. Pierre was. In order to do something while he lay in bed I sat down to write lyrics, thus becoming the Charles Aznavour I am today.

Actually, Pierre's seemingly indolent life was very well organised. At night he came back with a girl; when she left him in the morning he asked her to leave the key under the doormat. Then he turned on his other side. Later the next girl knocked on the door.

'The key's under the doormat,' he would call.

When the girl entered, he would gently ask her to get his breakfast ready, and when she had done so she was allowed to lie down beside him. He finished his breakfast before taking her into his arms.

In Lille we were much applauded. On our return to Paris Marquet had excellent news for us: Andrez, the great success at the Aiglon, was ill, and Roche and I would take his place. We would get the princely sum of eight hundred francs a night. I rushed home in the métro to tell my parents.

While we worked at the Aiglon we used to fetch Aida at the Concert Mayol after the performance, then dine at a small restaurant, Le Petit Chambord. Three pretty girls, who belonged to the stage too, sat nightly at the bar. Marquet

42

seduced one, I the second, and Roche the third. I have to admit that we behaved rather badly to achieve our ends.

Roche's parents were very upperclass people. They had a large flat in Paris with many rooms and many beds. Roche had his bedroom, his sister had hers, the parents theirs, and in the drawing room were plenty of sofas. The parents didn't come often to Paris. Generally they lived with the sister at Prelle in the Department of the Oise. So Roche's friends, who naturally included me, spent most of their nights in the flat, a matter of Ausweiss again. When the parents were tactless enough to come to Paris, which was usually in the morning, the sister telephoned to warn us. We jumped out of beds and off sofas, got dressed and sat around in the drawing room. When the parents arrived they were always astonished to see so many visitors so early in the day. Sometimes, it happened that the sister called us after the first warning to tell us they had missed the train. Everybody got back into bed.

Roche's parents never found out though this way of life lasted for seven or eight years.

To that flat we took the three girls who then had to spend the night with us as they had no Ausweiss. To entice them to the flat we had told them we were taking them to a new secret night club

My friend Pierre Roche was a remarkable man in every sense. He was never in a hurry to make use of anything he was given (women excepted). At the beginning of the war he was presented with a ham. He hung it in the lavatory as he wanted to keep it for an evil day. Somehow no day was evil enough to take the ham down. When the war was over the ham was full of maggots, and had to be thrown away.

He would eat noodles but without butter because the butter should wait for an evil day. We his friends used to steal a little of his butter. He never noticed it. All he said was he thought he had more. I was devoted to him, yet we were such a contrast: he tall and calm, I short and a bundle of nerves.

I never failed to go home to my parents in the day time to change and take a meal with them. Mother said with a sigh that I didn't look well. If I continued to spend my nights in my friend's flat I was sure to fall ill. I seldom felt fitter.

The only thing that annoyed me in the large flat was the well regulated visits of Roche's girl friends, and the hours and hours he spent in bed while I had to search for scores for our repertoire of songs. It wasn't too easy to find songs for two voices. The friends we asked to write chansons for us didn't come up with ideas we liked. One day in my irritation I remarked to Riesner, 'Surely it isn't witchcraft to write a song.'

'Witchcraft, witchraft,' he sneered. 'If it were so easy everybody would be writing songs. Try and see whether you can do it.'

I sat down and wrote my first lyrics with Riesner watching me, amused and sceptical. In the evening I asked Roche to set it to music, and the next day we submitted the song to our friends at the Club. Riesner was the one who was the most enthusiastic.

'Your song has a new style,' he said, 'a language of its own. I'm certain it'll go a long way.'

I wanted to persuade some great music hall star to sing it. I managed to see Edith Piaf who declined it, observing, 'It's too masculine. I couldn't sing it.'

I waited on Yves Montand in his dressing room at the Théâtre de Montparnasse. 'Not my style,' he said. Only Georges Ulmer agreed to sing it, and won with it the Grand Prix du Disque.

J'ai bu (I drank) was the title of the song.

> *I'm drunk*
> *And mad*
> *I see now that in spite of your caresses*

You were lying
I'm drunk
And yet I loved you as a true love
But one day in spite of my prayers you left me
Let's not talk about it
I'm drunk
I've quickly forgotten your caresses
I prefer myself in my drunkenness
And far from you
I'm drunk
The pavement is not big enough for me
And staggering I shout loudly
That the little cops are all my friends
And I drink

Slowly, Roche's and my name ceased to be unknown. Nevertheless, we were far from being famous. On the other hand, we got several engagements, and started on a new venture, singing not only in the Occupied Zone but in the Forbidden Zone too. The Forbidden Zone included all the towns near the Atlantic Wall. To visit them a special permit was needed, but we didn't apply for two reasons: the German authorities would have refused, and they might have sent us to work in Germany.

We had heard that there was a dearth of artistes in the Fobidden Zone since nobody was allowed into it. So we knew we would earn good money if we succeeded in getting in. Not only would we be well paid but we could bring back black market food since there was still plenty to eat in the country, whereas the poor Parisians were suffering from hunger. Few trains were bound for the Forbidden Zone, and to some towns there were no trains whatever. We had also heard that many bridges near the towns had been bombed by the Allies or sabotaged by Resistance workers, so when the trains approached the bridges they had to slow down. That was a vital piece of information inasmuch as it was too dangerous to alight at the stations in the towns, for we would be arrested at once for entering the Forbidden Zone without a permit. We accepted contracts only in towns that weren't far from a bridge.

We left Paris by train, and when the train slowed down before the bridge near the town I jumped, Roche threw me the suitcases, then jumped too. We hid till the train was out of sight. Then either on foot or in a bus we continued our journey to the town. We kept our eyes open: the farms we saw on the way would be visited on our way back to buy food to take to Paris. Now and then the farmers made us presents of eggs and butter.

In the Forbidden Zone we appeared even in towns like Le Havre.

We also sang in the Vendée and in Anjou. To reach the towns there we went on a bicycle, one for the two of us, the suitcases in front and behind us.

In Paris I now lived permanently with Roche, there being no room for me in my parents' flat. Very courageously father gave asylum to Russians who had been forced into the German Army, and to Jews on the run who were hoping to join the *Maquis* (the Resistance). There were nights when about twenty of them slept on mattresses in the flat. Father gave the Russians civilian suits which friends in the Resistance put at his disposal. It was my job to get rid of the uniforms.

During the curfew I would leave the house, carrying the dangerous parcel in the pitch dark night. I listened carefully. If I heard a German patrol I vanished back into the house. If I didn't I dropped my parcel into the first sewer opening.

However, one night I was caught by French policemen because I had no Ausweiss. Luckily I had no parcel either. They took me to the police station, where I had to spend the night in the company of other people who had been caught the same way as I. We were petrified the lot of us. If a German were killed in the course of the night the hostages would be chosen among poor fools like ourselves.

At five in the morning a policeman came to our cell to offer us coffee before letting us go. 'You're lucky,' he said. 'Nothing has happened in the night, so you can hop it.' I refused the cup of coffee. While I drank it a German might be killed, and a cup of coffee was hardly worth facing an execution squad!

There was also the famous incident when we were supposed to poison someone who was working with the Germans and the way chosen to do this deed was to get the man to eat a specially prepared dish of *civet de lapin* (rabbit stew). Everyone was terribly afraid that, my parents' generosity being well known, one of the other guests, coming into the apartment hungry, would help himself to the poisonous stew. In the event, I think the rabbit was thrown out and some other less hazardous method of dispatch was chosen for the German sympathizer.

One of my father's best friends at this time was the legendary Resistance hero Mamouchian. Poet and orphan, he taught me to play chess and involved the family with Parisian Resistance groups and sympathizers, Communists, Armenians and Jews, Mamouchian wrote his last letter from prison to his wife Melini to my father's house. We kept her hidden for a year. Aragon wrote his famous poem *L'Affiche Rouge* about Mamouchian's courage.

The Allied bombardments became so heavy that hardly any trains ran any more. Roche and I had to rely completely on our bicycle when we went on tour.

We undertook fairly long journeys on that bike. On one occasion we pedalled as far as Laval. Roche and I changed places every twenty kilometres or so. As I am short and he is tall we had to raise or lower the saddle every time we changed places. We slept in lofts, fed with the peasants, and ate ham, eggs and cheese again.

It took us two days to get to Saumur, where we remained for a fortnight, and were paid seven hundred francs a night. Roche wrote the music of our songs, I the lyrics, but I did try out tunes on the piano when I had the opportunity.

In Saumur I heard that Damia, who was engaged to

sing in Angers, couldn't come for lack of trains. I telephoned the director of the Angers theatre.

'How much will you offer us if we come?'

'Fifteen thousand francs each day.'

'How many days?'

'Two.'

'We're coming.'

I had lost my voice by the time we reached Angers. I took honey, then a hot lemonade, then milk, all of them of no avail. Even so we appeared, but the hard hearted director paid us only half the fee. 'I only got half the number,' was his excuse.

From Angers we cycled to Laval, from Laval to Le Mans. Before returning to Paris we bought four kilos of butter, three dozen eggs and a chicken. Loaded with them and our suitcases we did the 220 kilometres that separates Le Mans from Paris in one day.

Going on tour was risky and often useless in the last years of the Occupation. If there was any sabotage or other trouble with the townsfolk the theatres, cinemas and nightclubs were closed by order of the German authorities. Certainly the Occupation was no help to people in our profession.

My fundamental reason or inspiration for writing songs was based on my conviction that the French chanson, in fact the chanson all over the world, had insipid lyrics. There were of course some notable exceptions, but generally the chansons were inane. So when I wrote the words for Roche and me I wanted to do something new, more truthful and far more to the point. After Georges Ulmer had sung *J'ai bu* everybody began to ask me for a new song. I was willing, but Roche couldn't work as fast as I. So the moment came when I decided that I would have to try my hand at writing the music too. The next stage was words by Aznavour, music by Aznavour and Roche. I found the melody, he the harmony, and in time I learnt harmony, but mine was always a simple one.

However, in those years of Occupation I wasn't busy only with my profession. In fact, my first marriage was approaching, though slowly as will be seen. It all began on a night in the Petit Chambord restaurant near the Concert Mayol, at the time of the battle of Stalingrad in 1942. I noticed a lady seated at a table; I was sitting on a bar-stool. I went up to her, and put on my seducer act. She stopped me, saying, 'Don't waste your time. I'm flattered you take me for a young woman, but as a matter of fact I've a daughter aged sixteen. I'm here because of her as she wants to become a singer. I'm trying to get her an audition at the Concert Mayol. Do you know the director?'

'Most certainly, Jean Réna is a very amiable man, and knows his job. You can speak to him in all sincerity. I can give you an introduction to him.'

'You're very kind but it isn't worth it.'

'As you like.'

Next night the mother came again, accompanied this time by her daughter. I had liked the mother: the daughter I liked even more. Her name was Micheline, she had a charming face and a good figure. I was struck by her voice. It could have been the voice of an opera singer. I went up to their table.

'I remember you,' said Micheline. 'I saw you in a revue in Belleville.'

'Did you like it?'

'I thought you were very good.'

The ice was broken. The mother left the table for a moment, and I quickly asked her whether we could meet the next day. 'Without your mother,' I added.

'I'll try,' she said, 'but it'll be very difficult.'

'Tell her you're going for an audition.'

She thought that a good idea. In my fear of her mother returning before I fixed a date with her I spoke even faster. The result was that she agreed to meet me alone next afternoon. I told her I would take her to a fun fair.

She was punctual next afternoon, and we went to the fun fair and thus began our relationship that led us to marriage. I fell in love with her, such a different girl after the girls I had

49

known. No popping into bed with Micheline who was a girl of principles, and she kept to them. We contemplated seriously the idea of marriage. Her father was an antique dealer, separated from his wife; nonetheless the couple were both against it. On the other hand, my parents were for it. Micheline and I saw no reason why we should stay engaged as long as her parents suggested. Thanks to her excellent voice she got an engagement at the Concert Mayol. Her parents, however, continued to repeat we were too young to get married.

'If you still care for each other in two years' time,' said the mother, 'I'll agree to the marriage. You, Charles, must see more of the world before you settle down.'

She suspected me of being an assiduous pursuer of skirts.

I agreed to wait. I was so much in love that I would have agreed to anything to be able to remain near Micheline.

And while we waited the Normandy landing approached. Engagements were even more difficult to find. Nevertheless, Roche and I managed to get one first at the Théâtre de l'Étoile, then at the Excelsior. Theatres weren't allowed to use electric lighting at night, but both theatres had open roofs which helped a little. The star, of course, was given the full treatment, that is car headlights while he or she was on the stage. At the Étoile, Roche and I were number three—just enough light not to sing in complete darkness. But at the Excelsior we came on just after the star which was of no help at all. Darkness after light.

My parents were having trouble too. The Gestapo had raided their flat, looking for Mamouchian. He had attacked a German car in the rue Cadet, a car which carried a general and several sacks full of money. He and his friends got hold of the sacks, the attack lasting only a few seconds, and in full daylight with shopping housewives looking on. Mamouchian believed blindly in the Allied victory, and he was killed by the Germans only a short time before the Liberation.

The flat was crowded every night with members of the Resistance, one following the other. Three came if two left. Father and I moved into a small hotel opposite our house in the rue de Navarin. Every morning just before the end of the curfew the Gestapo burst into the flat, where all they found was mother and Aida fast asleep. The others had left long before. Once the Gestapo had gone father and I crossed the street, and had breakfast with mother and Aida.

The game was too dangerous, so father decided to send his wife and daughter to a friend in Yvetot in Normandy, and when he heard from them that they had arrived safely he sighed his relief. Then he had to flee to Lyons from the Gestapo.

Next day the Allies landed in Normandy in the Contentin quite near to Yvetlot. Mother and Aida had to drag themselves back to Paris, where they arrived hungry and exhausted.

Roche and I hadn't a sou left, and there was nothing to eat in Paris as no food arrived any more. The Petit Chambord had to close its doors like all other restaurants. Driven by hunger I decided to do something about it. Micheline was in tears when I told her I was going into the country to find food, any food, to keep us alive. 'It would be so stupid to get yourself killed a few days before the Liberation,' she moaned.

One has to survive to be liberated. So off I went, and came back with a sack of potatoes, weighing fifty kilos, not an easy task for a short person like me.

Father returned from Lyons which he had found more dangerous than Paris. The family was reunited, and this time it included Micheline who had come to stay with us. She shared a bed with Aida.

Then came the Liberation with church bells ringing, and the tricolour flying again.

I saw the Germans entering Paris; now I saw the Allied troops liberating the city. I stood in the crowd with Aida and Micheline as the American lorries filed past. The two good-looking girls were quickly noticed by the GIs who threw them rations and cigarettes from the lorries. At that time a packet of American cigarettes cost a hundred francs in the black market. Mind you, I did give each of the girls a packet of cigarettes, that is let them keep them. The rest was rushed to the black market.

Newspapers appeared again. I went to the Nouvelles Messageries, and was back in my old trade. I was asked to sell newspapers in the suburbs. I cycled to the suburbs with them. But I didn't have to sell papers for a long time. Gala performances and public dances mushroomed in the euphoria of the Liberation. Roche and I got an engagement in a Club in the rue Fontaine. When we were asked how much we wanted I took my courage in both hands, and said, 'Three thousand francs.' Indeed a big sum.

'Each of you?'

'Of course.'

'Nightly?'

'What else do you expect?'

'Very expensive.'

'We are expensive.'

It was accepted.

For the first time Roche and I were a real success. When Bardy, the director of the nightclub, decided to keep us on we asked for fifteen thousand francs a night, and that was accepted too. Roche and I were in seventh heaven. With the money we had posters made with our likenesses, got records made accompanied by Henri Lecca's orchestra. If only it could last!

It didn't. The great happy days of the Liberation turned into grey days of want with the war and the restrictions continuing.

Chapter Five

When the war was over lassitude crept upon most of us. Danger and hunger finally belonged to the past, but one had known too many privations to enter the future gaily. And when there is no money war time and peace time resemble one another. Roche and I were back on the road to the pawnshop.

Roche was offered the job of pianist in a small orchestra for the season in the casino of Saint-Raphael on the Riviera.

'What about me?' I said to the mutual friend who had offered the job.

'Do you play any instrument?'

'None.'

'In that case . . .'

'I could sing with the orchestra.'

'Our budget doesn't allow for a singer.'

Roche suggested I should play the bass.

'Are you mad? I've never touched that instrument in my life.'

'You'll learn to.'

'What, in a fortnight?'

'You will if you want to.'

I learnt to play the bass without any enthusiasm. I also learnt four dance tunes. Enough to make people dance on the floor of the casino I thought as I signed the contract.

I found a room in a boardinghouse in Saint-Raphael. I wired mother to come down there with Aida and Micheline. Came the opening night, I played the four dance tunes, but when no member of the management was in sight I sang with the orchestra. When any of them appeared I was back in the pit. One of them, who wasn't entirely deaf to music, asked me once why I always played the same tunes.

'Because the public likes them.'

'So often? Seems strange to me.'

'During the war people badly missed American tunes. Now they want them all the time. It's purely to please them that I play the same tunes again and again.'

Although he accepted my explanation I didn't feel at ease. So I said to Roche that the bass must disappear. However, I disappeared first in that I had an acute attack of appendicitis, and was rushed to hospital to be operated on. I was back a week later, but didn't touch the bass, explaining to the director that standing up was dangerous after an operation. Hower, singing wouldn't harm me at all. The director gave in, but there came a day when he made it clear that I was under contract to play the bass and I was now well enough to do so.

The next day I had to leave for Paris for my Army medicals. I asked my colleagues to get rid of the bass while I was away, and attend to that swiftly as I would be away for thirty-six hours. I left with a heavy heart because doing my military service would be catastrophic at that stage of my career. The medicos at the recruiting centre found nothing wrong with me. My heart was even heavier when I took train back to Saint-Raphael. (I wasn't called up in the end.)

Roche welcomed me with the happy tidings that a client had dropped the bass and broken it. 'Pretend to be furious,' Roche advised me. I gave a good imitation of it when I saw the director who told me with a sigh that the repair would take a considerable time there being but one stringed-instrument maker on the whole Riviera.

I went to see him, and begged him to take two whole

months to repair the instrument. He obliged, and I finished the season singing with the orchestra which was what I really wanted.

Back in Paris Roche and I chased round, trying to find an engagement. We were lucky in that we were engaged in a small troupe that was to tour Eastern France. Luckily too Micheline was taken on.

There was only one snag during the tour, namely that Micheline went to her bedroom after the performance and locked herself in. I was accustomed to that, but our colleagues jeered at me. In their world her behaviour was ridiculous and inexplicable. They thought me just as ridiculous for putting up with it. Admittedly, I was engaged to a saint, nevertheless the chaste life wasn't to my liking. Roche said I was pining away. In fact, I didn't feel up to form, and on the night of our return to Paris I joined him and our usual merry girlfriends after taking the saint back to her parents.

After that night I felt healthy again, and since women are creatures of intuition Micheline decided not to postpone our wedding any longer.

My parents were devoted to her. As I have said she lived in their flat for a time. It is an old Armenian custom to invite the son's fiancée to stay with her future parents in law. She became so much part of the family that she, the hundred per cent French girl, sang in Armenian with them all the operettas they loved to sing. She took part in all their activities.

Micheline and I had fifty francs for our wedding. I went to see the priest at the Armenian church, and put my case to him, a curious case because despite my possessing only fifty francs I wanted a nuptial mass with flowers, incense and the red carpet. The priest was a kind, understanding man who said there would be an expensive wedding on such and such a day. He would marry Micheline and me immediately after it, so there would still be flowers, tapers and a carpet in the church. So it happened, and I can say that ours was as fine a wedding as any rich man could ask for.

We returned to my parents after the wedding, and on the

following day I went on tour, alone, as my wife wasn't engaged. Verily it isn't easy to be an artiste's wife.

When I got back cousins of mine, who lived on the fifth floor of a house in the rue Louvois, told me a room was to be let on their floor. Micheline and I went to have a look at it. The window gave on a corridor, the window in the corridor on a dark courtyard. The room was small, and lacked running water, electric light and any kind of heating. As we had no alternative we took the room, and I turned into a skilled workman. I put in a sink, although the water had to be fetched from a tap in the corridor. A small portable stove followed because Micheline was an excellent cook who knew better than anyone I ever met how to cook my favourite dish, a potato ragout. Naturally, we had a bed, also two small chairs and a table bought at the flea market. I put in the electric light, and there was a wardrobe too but very little to hang in it as in our poverty we possessed only few clothes. Ours had to be a carefully disciplined life in our room in order not to fall over each other.

I thought the room perfection itself thanks to my efforts. Micheline wasn't of the same opinion. The life of Mimi Pinson didn't appeal to her. There were a thousand noises in the house which all seemed to rise up to our room, and at night the noise of the traffic was so loud that it was like living inside a car engine.

Ours was a Bohemian life, and Micheline wasn't made for it. In the first days she said she was delighted with the room and the work I had put into it. Then she escaped from it as often as she could, spending her time with my parents. When I escaped I went to see Roche in his flat.

He and I continued writing chansons. I had the sudden idea of calling a song *Trois filles à marier* (Three Daughters to Marry). Roche thought it a capital title, and we went to see Mme Legrand, a music editor, to offer it to her as we badly needed an advance.

'Too short,' she said.

We returned to Roche's flat, and came back to her with four daughters to marry. Still not long enough. We received our advance only when we presented her with five daughters to marry. *Cinq filles à marier.*

Then we went on tour again, and tired of our dark hole Micheline moved in with my parents.

Micheline was pregnant. Now no excuse was left for the dark hole. She remained with my parents while waiting for the baby, and I moved in with Roche. Because of his reputation that didn't please her too much, so I went to see her in my parents' flat three times a day.

Roche and I got a week's engagement at the Palladium. On the first night as I announced my chanson *J'ai bu* a man in the audience shouted that I was a liar, the song wasn't mine, it was by Georges Ulmer, and being a personal friend of his he had the privilege of being present when he wrote it. The audience took his side. Roche was imperturbable but I was livid. I shouted to the man that he was the liar, and probably hadn't seen even the shadow of Georges Ulmer. The man continued shouting. I sent a man to a nearby music shop, where I knew he could find the song. I told the spectators we would continue the programme while waiting for the proof. The audience hardly bothered to listen to us. At last the man was back with *J'ai bu*. It was shown to the spectators, and I said to the fellow who had called me a liar and himself a friend of Georges Ulmer, 'Keep it. It's a present. It gives the name of the one who wrote the song, and will teach you to keep your trap closed.'

'What does it prove?' he shouted.

But the spectators changed sides and warmly applauded us.

On 21 May 1947 our daughter Patricia Seida was born. My joy was immense. There was no more question of Micheline and the baby returning to the rue Louvois. I also wanted my daughter to have an Armenian background, so they continued living with my parents.

Roche and I were slowly forging ahead. We were considered as the avant-garde of the chanson, and singers in need of songs for their performances applied to us. No stars were among them, but some were beginning to make a name for themselves. A number of them made records with our songs, which was good for our reputation.

The telephone rang frequently in Roche's flat. Once, as I lifted the receiver a hoarse voice said, 'Mistinguett speaking. I hear you write modern songs. I'd like you to come round and show me some.'

Of course, I thought I was dealing with a practical joker, and said so.

'This is really Mistinguett speaking. I'm not joking when I say I want to meet you.'

Roche asked me who I was speaking to.

'A lunatic who wants me to believe she's Mistinguett,' I said.

'Hand me the receiver,' said Roche.

Yes, it was Mistinguett, and she invited us to see her the following day.

At two in the afternoon we appeared in her flat, all stucco and rococco, the way the stars of bygone days liked it. She showed us to the piano. We had only one free chanson, *Le Bal du faubourg* and she listened to it attentively.

'But,' she said, 'you have written the verses in the minor key and only the chorus in the major key.' We looked at her, astonished. 'You will have to put it all in the major key for me,' she said. 'You see, when I sing in the major key my cheeks go up—' she demonstrated '—and I look fine. If I sing in minor everything sags—like this—and it is horrible.'

She was as vain as anything, though she must have been nearly sixty at the time, but she was a great star who used to call Maurice Chevalier 'the little one' even though he was but ten years or so younger than herself. She deliberately forgot the names of younger stars.

'What's the name of the plain little undersized woman with a voice that's too big for her body?' she would ask us.

'Piaf?'

'Oh, that's it. Piaf.'

Mistinguett had a big mouth, a dark brown speaking voice, and 'the most beautiful legs in France'—a fact she never forgot. She had a great sense of humour. She was also reputed to be tight with money. There is a story of her meeting with Chevalier for a coffee and both of them sitting there for hours since neither of them was prepared to pay.

Mistinguett was really the original of such American stars as Fanny Brice. She could tear people up with words but my God she could capture the public when she sang. She could, quite simply, make them fall in love. She tried it on me when I was 21 and she was over sixty. She stood up in front of me and sang and the magic worked. While she was singing she had me in love.

Once when Mistinguett came to hear Piaf sing, which was a great honour, she was so old that she became very puffed going up the stairs. One of Piaf's people said to her, 'Imagine the publicity if Mistinguett died on coming up to see you.'

Another time when Roche and I went to see Mistinguett she took us up to the attic, where she showed us dresses she had worn on the stage in the course of her long career. In this one she had appeared in 1923, in that one she had had her immense success in *Mon homme*, the third she had worn when she had sung and danced with Chevalier. That went on for hours, and Roche and I really couldn't take it any more. As she had invited us to dinner, we went down to the flat, where we were joined by four old men, erstwhile young partners of the Mademoiselle.

After the salad with which the dinner had started, while Roche and I were eagerly waiting for a plentiful meat dish, she announced that meat was too heavy for an evening meal, so there would only be vegetables. After them she asked, 'Who wants cheese? I'm not taking any.'

The erstwhile young partners followed her example. Sadly Roche and I declared we wanted no cheese either.

After dinner we left her with her friends and their many memories, and ran to the nearest restaurant to have a proper meal.

Mistinguett was a great star of the music hall, but we decided our songs weren't for her. Piaf was our aim. If she agreed to sing a chanson of ours our cup of happiness would be full to the brim. For hers was the magic name in the world of the chanson. We tried to telephone her several times. Each time a secretary answered, saying if we had a chanson we thought was suitable for her we should send it, and if she liked it she would write to us. Neither Roche nor I liked offering songs to people we had no personal contact with, though once during the Occupation I had caught sight of Chevalier, at the métro station of the Opéra. Chevalier was the singer I admired most since my childhood. I went up to him, and handed him the score of one of my songs. Charmingly he took it, and left with it. I waited for a long time to hear from him. Not a word, and I became annoyed with my idol. Only years later did I find out that the reason he didn't get in touch with me was because I had forgotten to put my name and address on the score!

Roche and I were climbing slowly but surely up the ladder of recognition. In any case people began to know we were singers and not acrobats, which is already something. Roche and I appeared one night in the Salle Washington for a live broadcast. Piaf and Trenet were in the auditorium. There being no stage entrance in the Salle Washington spectators and performers came in through the same door. The performers sat in the audience, waiting for their turn on the stage. As the stage was narrow the piano was far behind me, giving me the impression that I was singing alone. That didn't help my stage fright caused by the presence of Piaf, Trenet and the Bretons. Moreover, ours was the first number. So there I was, facing the celebrities with Roche eight metres behind me.

I wanted to make a good impression, and as I sang I heard laughter, the sort of deep laughter that comes from the belly. It was Piaf who was laughing. She sat with her legs wide apart, her head thrown back. At the end of the song I turned to Roche, and said, 'It works.' Piaf was the first to applaud, and she was the first too after the second and third chanson.

When I left the stage and I was back in the auditorium Piaf waved to me, which meant she wanted to speak to me; so I shouldn't leave before the end. I waited timidly in a corner, and when the performance was over I didn't dare approach her. Timidity is often misunderstood, and is taken for arrogance. It was Piaf who came up to me, and asked in her inimitable way whether I was afraid of her. I admitted that I was a little. She seemed to like the idea of someone being afraid of her.

'You write your own songs?' she asked.

'I write the words, Roche the music.'

'Who's Roche?'

'My partner who sings with me.'

'I thought you sang alone.'

She hadn't noticed Roche way back on the stage. Then she asked why I had never shown her any of my songs. I assured her I had tried but didn't succeed in getting into her presence. She wanted to know what I was doing that night.

'I'm going home to my wife,' I answered.

'Another who's married,' she said. 'You're all idiots. Let her wait for once. She'll have to get accustomed to it. She'll start now. Come with us.'

(It is impossible to translate Piaf's language into English. It was picturesque and vulgar, yet always witty.)

I insisted on taking Roche along. He and I were deeply moved to be able to go through a door we had believed was closed to us. Among the privileged few in her drawing room I met Marguerite Monnod and Henri Contet. Except for Roche and me they were all close friends which made me feel awkward. They were trying to make us out, to tabulate us. Moreover, Roche deserted me, sitting down at the other end of the drawing room beside a young woman with long hair whose name was Faon and who was Piaf's secretary. I hardly dared to move.

Suddenly, Piaf asked, 'Are you a Jew?'

'No, I'm of Armenian origin.'

'What's that?'

'Too long to explain.'

'Then don't.'

I thought the ordeal was over.

'Why are you dressed in mourning?' she fired at me.

'Because it's less conspicuous when my shirt is dirty.'

'Perhaps your shirt is dirty this moment.'

'That's possible.'

She turned to her friends, 'But he's OK, this little fellow. He even wears dirty shirts.'

Everybody approved of her words. I was examined, and I knew it depended on that whether I would be admitted to her intimate circle or not. My shirt being dirty was definitely in my favour. I felt I was half accepted, and was glad to see that the scrutiny was over.

'Tell me the story of your life,' Piaf said.

I told it. Impressed by my past in the streets and in the bals musettes which was rather like her own, she asked whether I knew how to valse. I said I did, she said she would see in a moment if I lied. She ordered Roche to sit down at the piano, and play a valse musette.

When Roche began to play a valse musette Piaf rose from her chair.

'Sit down,' I ordered her.

And she understood since the street and public dances were as much her background as mine. I whistled as the gutter-snipes do. It wasn't for me to go to her: it was for her to come to me. No politeness or good manners exist in that world. It wasn't the famous Edith Piaf who rose to go to the unknown little singer: it was the girl who was called to dance by her man. She looked delighted as I put my arm round her waist. While I danced with her I felt as powerful as a giant, and at that moment I didn't care a damn what she thought of me as an artiste, but I did care a great deal of what she thought of me as a dancer in the style she liked. After fifteen minutes it was she who gave in because she was out of breath. We were loudly applauded.

Then I danced the paso doble with her. Then she wanted to dance the tango, the authentic popular tango as danced in public dances. I think we danced the tango that lasted the longest since the beginning of time.

'Come back tomorrow,' she said when we were leaving at last. 'I want to speak to you seriously.'

Roche and I missed the last métro because of the late hour. We slept side by side on a bench.

Next morning I rang Piaf's bell. Faon opened the door, and said Mademoiselle was still asleep.

I waited for two hours. At the end of this I was taken into her bedroom. Impervious of my presence she was busy putting vaseline into her nostrils. Then she wiped her fingers on her nightdress.

'Have you had breakfast?' she asked.

'Yes, I have.'

'Really?' she shouted.

'Really.'

'Tell me frankly because if you're hungry it's bloody stupid to say you're not.'

Again I assured her that I had breakfasted, so she ate her breakfast, smearing the honey on her nightdress and sheets. Then she told me why she wanted to see me. She was going on tour with the Compagnons de la Chanson. Roche and I could be the first act in the programme. After our number I would announce hers.

I thought I would have to announce the Compagnons de la Chanson too, but she said she would do that. Then I made a blunder: I asked her how much she would pay us, which was the last thing one should ever have asked her. She stared at me, then she exploded, and her wrath was awful. To explode like that was a special trait of hers.

She called me every name under the sun. I had been honoured to be invited to join her troupe, and all I could think of was money. The whole population of Paris would kiss her feet if she allowed it to take part in her concert. Everybody would consider it the chance of a lifetime. She was shouting, throwing her arms about.

'Don't get angry,' I said. 'One must live, and I've a wife and child to keep.'

As I have said the idea of my being married didn't appeal to her.

'Do you think I've nobody to keep?' she shrieked. 'Had anyone made me the offer I just made you when I begged in the streets I'd have kept my trap closed and jumped to it. And if I'd opened my trap it would have only been to say thank you.'

'Thank you.'

'Yes thank you, or no thank you?'

'I thank you on my behalf. I must ask Roche.'

'You're not big enough to take your own decisions.'

She inveighed against Roche, the aristocrat, who was probably still asleep, who didn't deign to come and see her. Why didn't he send his valet? She ended our tête à tête, saying we were leaving for Roubaix on the sixteenth of the month, Roche and I would be paid what she felt like paying us, and we would have to obey her in every sense. The train left at 8.20, so we should be on the station platform at eight sharp. She loathed people who were unpunctual. In the meantime I could come to the house as often as I felt like it. Then she told me to scram because she was getting up.

Thus in less than twenty-four hours Piaf had become the biggest influence in my life, and that influence was to last for many years. I ought to stress here that I was the one man near her who never had a love affair with her, and in a sense this brought me even closer to her. For ours was a very close relationship, and it has survived her death, and her essence will remain with me for the rest of my life.

She was a phenomenon both as a person and as an artiste. She was aggressively proud of her poor origins, yet most of her lovers came from different backgrounds. She had never lived with a working man or a working man's son. Her mother was a singer and a dope addict who left Piaf's father and ended up singing in the street. Her father was a street acrobat and Piaf used to say that he worked in the streets because he was too good and too original for the circus. Actually, I suspect that the truth was the other way round and that the father was not talented but that her mother was. The proof after all, is Piaf herself. Singers do generally inherit their talent:

my father was a wonderful singer and Liza Minelli's mother *was* Judy Garland.

Piaf was a heavy drinker, but she knew how to hold her drink. She was an extraordinary creature even where drink was concerned. She knew exactly when to stop. Or when not to. She swore one night that she would give up drink for a whole year. She took that oath in the drawing room, and when I found her drinking heavily in the kitchen she said in that sincere voice of hers that she had taken the pledge in the drawing room, not in the kitchen, and I could see myself that she didn't touch a single drink in the drawing room.

During one of her abstemious periods we went one night to a restaurant. She started her meal with melon and port wine. 'You can't,' she said, 'have melon without port in it.' Half a bottle of port was poured over the melon. When she had finished it she said, 'The melon was excellent. I'll have another.' The other half of the bottle was poured over the second melon. It wasn't drinking: it was eating melon.

Nowadays there is television which shows young artistes how their famous colleagues live and work. At the time I entered Piaf's orbit it wasn't as easy as that for the beginners. They had to go to the theatre to see, watch and hear their betters. But to go to the theatre money was needed. I had the immense luck to see, watch and hear Piaf in her house and on the stage. I saw her at work, watched her preparing her repertoire of songs, choosing them, discussing them with their authors, saying she didn't like this line, or that line didn't suit her. Or telling them to change the music. In short, I learnt from her all you have to know in our profession.

She lived with her chansons, they became part of her. That total dedication of hers was the strongest influence I ever had in my career.

Yet I never was one of her real song writers. Her favourites and great successes were in a more popular vein, like *Le Légionnaire* for instance. I did write a few songs for her, and she liked them because they were so different from the songs she generally sang. Anyhow, it was Piaf herself who wrote her famous *La vie en rose*, and she also wrote beautiful lyrics for the first songs of Yves Montand.

After Piaf's offer to take Roche and me on tour with her I went straight to Micheline to tell her about it.

Our married life was in every sense a love affair between two very young people. We laughed and enjoyed ourselves. We loved going out with friends who led a similar existence. Fortunately mother looked after Patricia. It wasn't that Micheline didn't want to, but you can't drag a baby with you when you go out at night.

There was our work too. Micheline sang in one club, I in another, and after the performance we met up, and went to small bistros that weren't expensive to spend the rest of the night with friends. When I told her that Roche and I were going on tour with Piaf she congratulated us on our luck, but observed that Piaf was known to take possession of anybody who entered her orbit. To reassure her I said Piaf was after Roche. Micheline said I had told her the same after we had gone to see Mistinguett.

When the day of departure came, I had to shake Roche to get him out of bed. I hadn't forgotten what Piaf had said about punctuality. Of course, we couldn't find a taxi, and we raced with our luggage to the Gare du Nord that luckily wasn't too far from Roche's flat. We reached it just in time to see our train, the train that carried Piaf and the troupe, pulling out of the station. A real catastrophe, and it wasn't difficult to imagine Piaf's fury and rage. We stopped a railway employee to ask him when the next train left for our destination. Not before the evening. We explained it was a matter of life or death for us, so he suggested a goods train that was leaving in a few minutes, but it was going only as far as Amiens. Never mind, we rushed along the lines till we found the goods train. However, it was already moving. We made a last effort, and jumped into a truck with our luggage.

Our missing Piaf and the train was all Roche's fault as he hadn't got up in time. I told him so, but it was a waste of breath because he was sleeping calmly in a corner of the truck as befits one who has nothing to reproach himself with.

In Amiens we took a taxi to Lille. In Lille we climbed into a tram with all our luggage. The tram took us as far as Tourcoing, where we imagined Piaf's train had arrived hours ago. Great was our relief when the station master told us that the train we had missed in the morning would arrive in five minutes time. So we had reached Tourcoing before Piaf.

'You see there was no need to get upset,' said Roche, and we went and sat down on a café terrace opposite the station. We could see anybody who came out of the station from that vantage point. We had just finished our drink when Piaf and the troupe appeared. When she was only a few feet from us she said to Barrier, her impresario, in a voice that should have made us tremble, 'Let me never set eyes on them again. I gave them the one great chance of their lives, and the idiots didn't take advantage of it.'

Then she saw us. 'What the hell are you doing here?' she grunted.

'We're having a drink. Come and join us.'

She sat down with us. She wanted to be angry, but she couldn't resist having a good laugh.

The tour began. Before she came on, it was I who announced her, always with the same words. 'Only one name, and in that name the chanson itself: Edith Piaf.'

We did the North of France, and everything went well there. We moved on to Switzerland, and nothing went well there. We had money troubles too. Piaf said, 'Charles and I can always fall on our feet, singing in the streets, but the others will have to be repatriated if things continue like this.'

The Compagnons de la Chanson were serious people who kept their distance from revellers Roche and me. However, Piaf enjoyed our way of life. We always drank together, and I remember one of those serious Compagnons observing one night that Piaf was so tired and overworked that she couldn't stand on her feet any more.

From Switzerland we went to Liège, where Piaf had to leave us to go to Sweden for several gala performances. Her impresario had taken good care there shouldn't be any bottles in her luggage.

'Is it all arranged?' she whispered to me as she kissed me goodbye.

I assured her it was, and truly enough Roche and I had hidden bottles and bottles of beer in the pockets of her furcoat and under the mattress in her sleeping compartment. She knew she could trust us.

When she arrived in Sweden she sent me a cable. 'I would never have believed that I could miss you so much. Your little sister of the pavement, Edith.'

The next time Roche and I saw her she was preparing to go to America.

'It would be fun if you two could join me in America,' she said.

'We dream of the States, but haven't the money to get there,' we said.

'Be men,' she said. 'Find your way to America, and once you are there I'm sure you'll get on. Anyhow, I'll help you in America.'

'It's easy to say, be men,' I growled.

'Are you afraid of adventure?' said Piaf.

'Not us,' we said.

Later I told Roche that I had an idea, and if it came off we could go to the States.

It was 1948.

Chapter Six

The idea took me to Raoul Breton, the music publisher. Roche accompanied me. In the waiting room was a piano; Charles Trenet had often played on it. When we were ushered into Breton's presence, he said, 'I've been waiting for you for three months.'

'We were on tour with Piaf.'

He bade us sit down, then asked whether we had any songs to offer him. Yes, we had one, only one, but it would be sung by Piaf.

'She always says that,' Breton said. 'Still, let me hear it.'

He heard it and liked it. He said it was excellent, and was sure she would sing it. What were our terms?

'A hundred and eighty-one thousand francs,' I brazenly said.

Roche gasped. Breton said nobody had asked for such a large advance before.

'I don't say the contrary,' I said, 'but you could give it as a general advance on all future songs.'

'Pray, why that enormous sum of a hundred and eighty-one thousand francs?' Breton inquired.

I explained that when Piaf had told us that she was going to America she had challenged us to follow her. The hundred and eighty-one thousand francs was the sum we needed to fly to New York.

Breton looked at us pensively, then said in a resigned voice that he was as mad as us, and made out a cheque for that exorbitant sum.

We went to the nearest travel agency: no tickets for New York. All seats were booked in advance for several weeks. We tried other agents, eventually the KLM came to our rescue. We would fly to New York from Amsterdam.

'Is that all we need?' we asked the air line employee after we had paid for our tickets.

'Everything's all right now,' he assured us.

It wasn't so all right because when we got to Amsterdam we discovered that the reservations hadn't been made. It was almost impossible to find a hotel room as the town was packed with people on account of the coronation of Queen Juliana. Every day I rushed to the airfield while Roche either slept or chased some fair haired Dutch girl. On the fifth day we were told we could leave.

We were inside the plane ready to take off when a hostess appeared and called our names. We lifted our hands.

'The company is very sorry,' she said, 'but you have to get off the plane because the two people whose seats were given you have just turned up.'

'Out of the question,' I said.

'But, Monsieur . . .'

No but Monsieur for me. We had waited long enough. I shouted and made such a loud scene that even Roche, who was accustomed to my losing my temper, was astonished by it. The pilot came to find out what the noise was about.

'This passenger isn't willing to get off the plane,' said the hostess in a placid voice.

The pilot decided to keep us, and I sighed my relief. Our five days stay in Amsterdam had eaten into our reserves, leaving us with four dollars and eighty cents.

New York. We were touching down in the town Roche and I had been dreaming about. We would stroll on Broadway, we would see extraordinary shows, meet stars we had been admiring from a distance, hear jazz at every street corner and be able to go to Harlem with its musicians and singers of the blues. In short, we would see everything and have the time of our lives. And contracts would simply drop into our laps!

We felt great as we approached the immigration officers. We handed them our passports.

'Visas?' they asked.

'Visas? What visas?'

The officer spoke to us in English which neither of us could speak though we did understand the word visa, and he repeated it several times.

'Nobody spoke to us about visas,' I said to the immigration officer who didn't know a word of French. 'Had we been told that a visa was necessary we would have got it.'

He shook his head, then continued speaking in English.

'You learnt English at school,' I said to Roche. 'Here's your chance to speak it.'

'They speak American. That's not the same,' said Roche.

Our euphoria was over. Would they send us back to France by the first plane? The man who had spoken to us took us to another official who spoke a little Franch.

'How did you manage to get here without a visa?' he asked.

'I don't know.'

'Have you a return ticket?'

'No.'

'Have you enough money to buy one?'

'No.'

'Why did the two of you come here?'

'Mme Edith Piaf, the famous French singer, has asked us to join her over here.'

'Where is she?'

'In New York.'

'New York is big. Got her address?'

'We haven't, but we know that of her agent.'

His name was Fisher, but as we didn't know his initials several Fishers were tried on the telephone before the official got the right one. The news couldn't have been worse. Piaf was in Canada for ten days, and the impresario was with her.

The official then tried the French Consulate, but the office was closed already as it was getting late. We were locked up in a room till a tall man, who didn't speak a word of French, came to take us to a large car, and we were driven off in it. You couldn't open the doors from the inside, not that it mattered as we were too tired and downhearted to attempt to escape. One thing was sure: there would be no Broadway and no Harlem for us that night.

We drove for a considerable time before being taken on board a ferry which took us to Ellis Island, where the car stopped in front of an immense building. Two enormous fellows took us into an office. When the formalities were over they pushed us into a dormitory. We were in prison, not exactly the America we had dreamed of.

In the morning we were wakened by a babble of voices. Every possible language was spoken in the dormitory. Polish, Italian, Spanish, Yiddish, and Greek. English was the only language we didn't hear. There were no doors, even the lavatories hadn't any. We were led to the refectory, where there was plenty of food, but it all looked repugnant. I saw a big bowl of rice, and pointed at it.

'Just for the Chinese,' said the man in charge.

I pointed at a bottle of milk.

'You're not a baby.'

After breakfast the lot of us were locked into a vast room. In a corner stood a piano that was locked too. Roche asked the jailer to unlock it which he promptly did. When we opened it a whole procession of cockroaches emerged, and helped by some of our fellow prisoners we hunted them till none was left. Then Roche sat down at the piano to the delight of all present, and we spent the day playing and singing.

On the third day we were driven in a similar car to some court of justice, where a judge helped by an interpreter questioned us.

'Why have you come to America?' asked the judge.

'Our great dream during the war was to visit America when the war ended.'

'Do you belong to any political party?'

We said we didn't.

'What's your profession?'

'Author, composer and singer.'

'What have you written?'

I remembered that to amuse myself I had translated the lyrics of a song in an American musical which was still running on Broadway, *Finian's Rainbow*. I said to the judge that I had come to New York to meet the author to show him the translation. The judge became interested, or should I say curious? He asked me to sing a few words of that song which I promptly did. He stopped me with a gesture, then he applauded. He declared he found us sympathetic, and would do something to help us.

'The judge,' said the interpreter, 'grants you a visa for a short stay. Once you find work you must come here to have the visa extended. If you don't find work you'll have to leave the country.'

Roche and I thanked the judge from the bottom of our hearts.

We were taken back to Ellis Island, and were released the next day. We took a taxi, and I tried on the driver the only sentence I knew in the English language: 'I am very glad to meet you.'

'So what?' he said.

I handed him a piece of paper with Fisher's address on it. It was in Times Square. Roche and I were overcome by the sight of Times Square. Here you are nobodies it seemed to say to us, and nothing will be easy for you.

We weren't received with open arms in Fisher's office. He himself was still in Canada with Piaf.

'How much money have you got?' they asked us.

'Not much.'

'Where are you staying?'

'Nowhere. Our luggage is downstairs.'

We weren't making a good impression.

Eventually they sent us to a cheap hotel in 44th Street, the Longwell Hotel, which was the gathering point in New York of all European artistes who hadn't enough money to pay for their lodgings. Roche and I didn't know that, and on our way to the hotel we had one fear, namely that we would have to pay in advance, which of course we simply couldn't do. Our faces lit up as we entered the hotel lounge, for we heard French spoken. Many of the hotel guests were French. We immediately made the acquaintance of Lucien Jarraud, an acrobat who acted as our interpreter at the reception desk. Fourteen dollars a week for the two of us. Jarraud assured us we couldn't find anything cheaper in New York, so we took the room.

It wasn't much of a room what with the cracked washbasin and the radiator that whistled like a railway engine. Still, we felt relieved because no advance payment had been asked.

Roche and I left the luggage in our room, then went out to have a look at New York. We strolled along Broadway, and stopped outside a cinema. I have forgotten the title of the film which in any case didn't mean anything to us, but there was Gene Krupa and his orchestra in the interval. The tickets cost one dollar fifty cents each, a lot of money with our meagre resources.

'We won't be any richer if we don't go in,' I said.

So in we went, and stayed for several performances, enjoying Krupa and his orchestra and hardly bothering about the film. When we came out each of us had a hot dog for fifteen cents and a coca cola for five. Thus ended our first free day in the town of our dreams.

Raoul Breton had suggested we see Lou Levy of the Leeds Music Corporation who was a friend of his. In the morning we repaired to the Leeds Music Corporation. A secretary asked us whom we wished to see. Mr Lou Levy. What was our profession? Writing songs and music. Who were we? Roche and Aznavour. So far so good, and we were taken into the office of a tall man who received us most amiably. He was Lou Levy. Roche and I were proud of our English, so easy too, till Levy asked, 'How is the Marquise?' We both thought that he was

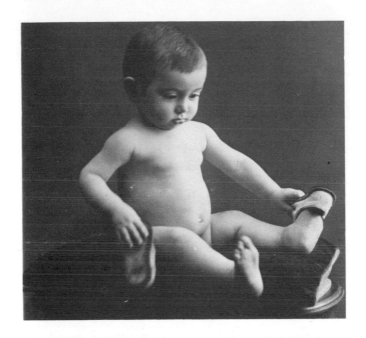

Above: Charles as a baby
Below: Mother, father, Charles and sister Aïda

Above: Charles' mother
Below: Charles' first cigarette—lit by sister Aïda

Charles, aged 3, with his grandmother, mother and Aïda

STUDIO EDOUARD

CARLET AINÉ

Above: Charles, aged 12, at the Théâtre du Petit Monde
Below: Charles as a young man

Above: Charles with Pierre Roche on piano
Below: Edith Piaf

Above: Charles, bandaged up after a serious car accident. He is with
Gilbert Bécaud
Below: Sitting on the steps outside Carnegie Hall, New York

Above: Séda, Charles' eldest daughter
Below: On his wedding day to Swedish born Ulla, with Sammy Davis Jnr and George Garvarentz next to Charles, and Petula Clark and Aïda next to Ulla. Las Vegas, 1967

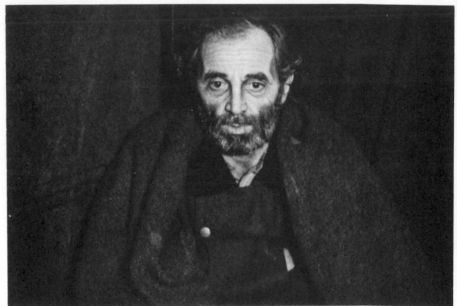

Above: Charles with Charlie Chaplin and his wife, Oona
Below: Charles as he appeared in *Blockhouse*, a film which was never shown in England

thinking of the popular chanson, *Tout va très bien Madame de la Marquise* which had been a great success before the war, hence was dated.

'Old,' I said. 'Oh, very, very old.'

Lou Levy looked at me in surprise. Had I said the wrong thing? I certainly had as I didn't know that Raoul Breton's wife was known among her friends as the Marquise. It took Levy a few more minutes to realise that we didn't know any English. Laughing loudly he summoned an assistant of his who spoke French fluently. We put our case to him, he translated it into English, Levy laughed a lot more before buying two of our songs for two hundred dollars.

Roche and I felt like millionaires. We paid the hotel for three weeks in advance, and the rest went on going to shows, visiting the town, eating hot dogs and buying a portable radio. And then we were broke again.

We weren't unduly worried since Piaf would be back from Canada any day now. However, what we didn't know was that she was at the moment madly in love with Marcel Cerdan, the world famous French boxer, and when she was in love she hadn't time to think of anybody or anything else.

I became very friendly with the hotel guests who were mostly French and Italian. We took to playing poker, a game that suits me perfectly, and generally I win at it. Moreover, at the Longwell there wasn't any danger of losing too much since the other gamblers were nearly as broke as Roche and Aznavour. We played with counters, and the maximum one could win was a beer or a Seven Up or a coca cola. Jarraud and I always chose coca cola as you got two cents back if you returned the bottle, whereas you got nothing for an empty beer bottle. As I won regularly I had enough two cents to buy a case of coca cola, and invited the losers to drink coca cola with me, which they found handsome and generous.

Roche, Jarraud and I added up our gains one evening, and the three of us were the lucky owners of three dollars and twenty-five cents, truly a princely sum. We were invited by Walter Pitchon, a new acquaintance, to a party given by some wealthy people. As Roche was the most cautious among us and was far from being a spendthrift, we gave him the three dollars and twenty-five cents for safe keeping before going to the party.

It was a sumptuous party with all the drinks and food one could dream of, and packets of cigarettes lay on every table. Unfortunately (as will be seen) there was also a very pretty girl at the party, and Roche made straight for her. She noticed his family coat of arms on his signet ring, and impressed as much by him as the coat of arms she took him away from the party. 'I'll be back soon,' Roche said before they left.

Jarraud and I left too after we had drunk, eaten and smoked to our hearts' content, walked back to the Longwell, and went to bed. Next morning Roche wasn't back and he wasn't back in the afternoon either. In fact, he stayed away for three days, and as he had our three dollars and twenty-five cents on him we starved for three days. On the fourth day he telephoned to ask us how we were keeping.

'We're dying of hunger, we haven't eaten for three days.'

'Then come along, the fridge is full,' he said.

'But how will we get there? I repeat we haven't a cent.'

'You'll manage,' he said, and gave the address which was in 79th Street, and rang off.

We went on foot to 79th Street, it was nearer to flying so hungry were we. Roche received us in a fine dressing gown, the châtelain welcoming his guests. The luxurious apartment was worthy of him. Our hostess offered us small, thinly cut sandwiches which we swallowed in a jiffy. Our hunger wasn't relieved.

'If you want anything more,' said the young woman who was strikingly good looking, 'go to the fridge.'

That was the last thing she should have said. Jarraud and I nearly emptied the fridge, stuffing ourselves.

'Don't overdo it,' said Roche, slightly ashamed of us.

'It's easy for you to talk. You had decent meals while we died of starvation.'

When Jarraud and I had eaten as much as we could we returned to the drawing room, sat on a divan, and took part in the conversation till we fell asleep. We woke up two hours later. The girl and Roche were talking quietly. I took the three dollars twenty-five cents off Roche, and Jarraud and I left without bothering too much about the impression we had made on our hostess.

In our hotel there stayed Florence and Frédéric, dancers both of them, and I had known them in France. In time Frédéric became a big name in show business, but when we ran into each other at the Longwell he wasn't famous yet. His full name is Frédéric Apkar, and he is of Armenian origin. When I had explained our situation to him and Florence they promised to get us an audition in some downtown cabaret or night club.

While we waited for the audition Roche and I went to a bar called Snooky to spend our last remaining cents. A pleasant man, who had overheard us speaking French, invited us to his table. He said he loved France, such a wonderful country, and he simply longed to visit it again. He hailed from Boston, and was in New York for a few days to see his parents who lived in Brooklyn. He swore he would look after us during his stay in New York.

He took us to different night clubs. Towards two o'clock we landed in one, where everybody, including porter and barman, sang songs. The cook too. Our new friend was called Victor, and he implored us to go to the pianist and ask him to let us play and sing just for a little while because he very much wanted to hear us sing in French. He didn't have to ask us twice since Roche and I were sadly missing our duets of old.

Next day he took us to his parents in Brooklyn. The father explained to me a roulette system with which he had nearly won in Monte-Carlo. He had perfected it since then, and at his next visit to Monte-Carlo he felt he was bound to win.

Victor continued to take us out, heaping food and drink on us, enjoying our company, swearing eternal friendship. Then suddenly he disappeared, and we never heard from him again.

Piaf returned from Canada on the day of Victor's disappearance. Somebody or other must have told her of our plight because she seemed to know everything that had happened to us since we landed in America. Oh, she loved us all right when we went to see her, but there was no enthusiasm in it, and I had the impression that we were in the way. She thought only of Cerdan. I couldn't resist reminding her that our coming to America had been her idea, but it wasn't the moment to mention it. In brief, she had no time for us, but as she wasn't the person to drop friends she said she was ready to help on the condition we didn't interfere with her private life, that is to say with her and Cerdan.

'While I was in Canada I mentioned you two to people who can help you. Go to Montreal, and you'll get an engagement at the Quartier Latin there the moment you arrive.' She held out her hand. 'Now buzz off both of you, I don't want too many people in the apartment because their presence would distract Cerdan who has to concentrate on his next fight.'

As we left Roche said not without irony that indeed we should keep away from Piaf, for if he lost the fight it would certainly be our fault. I felt bitter. I hadn't expected her to receive us like that.

However, that was Piaf. Whatever she did she did with all her might, and nothing could sidetrack her while she was at it. Marcel Cerdan followed her everywhere while she was on tour in America. She, who'd had practically no education whatever, decided to educate Cerdan. For instance, when she had to go out she left him with some serious book, saying, '*Mon chéri*, read this book, and you'll tell me what you think of it when I come back.' Cerdan read hard—he did anything she asked him to do—and when she returned they discussed the book at length. She wanted to improve his table manners too. '*Mon chéri*, you don't hold a fork like that,' and so on. It shouldn't be forgotten that she had done her apprenticeship in the same fashion, but let's face it: she didn't know much more than he.

When they were in Paris and he went into training Piaf

stayed at home, waiting for him like any boxer's wife. She even washed his linen.

As part of Cerdan's education she insisted on taking him to the Niagara Falls. As she hadn't seen them either she thought it would be an education for her too. They arrived at the Niagara Falls, she looked, then said, 'Just a lot of water,' and took Cerdan back to the hotel.

After Roche and I had left her we were crestfallen. We walked back to our hotel, where good news awaited us in that Frédéric and Florence had obtained an audition for us at the Café Society in Greenwich Village.

They kindly accompanied us so that we shouldn't be too frightened. Barney Josephson, who ran the Café Society, engaged us after he had heard three of our chansons. Our contract was for three weeks that included Christmas and the New Year, at three hundred and fifty dollars a week, and a hundred more if he kept us on at the end of the three weeks. We were to sing in the Café Society one night before our engagement to see the public's reactions, and then we could modify our repertoire of songs according to that. The trouble was that we were still in October, which meant that Christmas was a long way off.

We called Piaf to tell her we were ready to go to Montreal. She answered that she would arrange it for us.

The Compagnons de la Chanson had just got back from their Canadian tour, and were staying at the Longwell. I asked them what Canada was like. They said Canada was a fine country.

'I don't mean the landscape,' I said. 'I mean the girls.'

'I don't think you'll have any difficulty with them.'

I left them reassured, and when I repeated to Roche what they had said about the girls he became enormously keen on leaving for Canada as soon as possible.

Now we had an excuse to call on Piaf every day to find out more about Canada. Cerdan was invariably present, and to amuse us and even more himself he boxed with us a little, which Piaf didn't like because we made too much noise. One afternoon Cerdan said to me, 'Hit me as hard as you can.' I went for him, tried as hard as I could, but it was impossible to get through his defence. He was greatly amused, and when I had lost my breath he asked Roche and me to sing some of our songs—which was easier than boxing.

When the four of us went out Piaf was deeply impressed by people recognising the great Marcel Cerdan. 'He's somebody, isn't he?' she said happily, quite forgetting that she was somebody too.

When she noticed we were feeling at ease with her again she sent us packing at once. 'Aren't I entitled to be alone with Marcel?' On the night of his fight with Tony Zale she didn't turn up. It was too much for her to see the loved one fighting. But we were told to go, and were told by her at the same time that Cerdan and some friends would come to her apartment after the fight, her voice implying that we weren't included.

The following day she informed us that Montreal was all arranged. 'The Canadians offer you a contract for four weeks at three hundred and fifty dollars a week. You start in five days time. Now scram.'

We thanked her and scrammed. The same evening we tried out our chansons in front of the audience in the Café Society. Josephson said when we arrived, 'The French are doing very well in New York. Piaf and Jean Sablon are a great draw. I suggest you start with a typically Parisian chanson.'

Roche and I began with *Bal du Faubourg*, which couldn't have been more typically Parisian. The audience burst into laughter. They thought we were American singers imitating French singers. Though they soon discovered we were authentically French the harm was done, and we didn't manage to make a success of our performance. However, Josephson was reassuring. He said it would work, but we should write some songs in English before Christmas, and then everything in the garden would be lovely.

Chapter Seven

Roy Cooper was the name of the impresario who got us our Montreal contract. He met us at the airport, and told us we would be interviewed by the CKVL, a radio station that specialised in French songs and gave them a lot of publicity. In Montreal everything French is admired, and all artistes who come from France are acclaimed. Every Frenchman is assailed with questions about the mother country of two-hundred and more years ago.

'Roche and Aznavour,' asked the radio reporter, 'what do you think of Canada?'

'Let's get there first,' I answered.

Roche and I expected to enter a world of trappers and woodcutters. Instead we saw a modern town with more traffic than in Paris. We were greatly amused by the notices in two languages, such as: hot dog, *chien chaud*; cocktail, *coquetel*. And the French accent was so different from ours.

We were taken to The Tourist Room in Mountain Street: rue de la Montagne, where rooms had been booked for us. Once again we were assailed by questions. What were Chevalier, Tino Rossi and Charles Trenet doing? And the latest French films, and Jean-Paul Sartre's latest book? The Tourist Room was opposite the Quartier Latin, where we were to open the next night.

Roche was in ecstasy, for he had never before seen so many pretty girls. Montreal, he declared, was the town for him.

Our success was unbelievable. Neither Roche nor I had heard such thundering applause before. We were called back again and again, and it was Roche and I who tired first. We were out of breath while they continued clapping and shouting for us. I was perspiring hard, and a spectator handed me a handkerchief. Then the whole audience rose to applaud us even louder.

The papers praised us, and every night the nightclub was chockablock. We were offered an extra week, which we accepted on the condition that we were paid a hundred dollars more. Immediately this was agreed upon.

We had equal success with women. We led a gratifying life in every sense, going to parties after our performance in the Quartier Latin, often not returning to The Tourist Room before eight in the morning. Among the girls we met there was one, so Roche related the next day, who said her prayers on her knees before getting into his bed.

'She prayed for her soul before entering Hell,' I observed.

There being no success like success, an important looking man appeared in our dressing room one night. His name was Edmond Martin and he offered us a contract in his cabaret, Le Faisan Doré, for three months. How much did we want?

'Five hundred dollars.'

He said that was too much as all he could afford to pay us was four hundred dollars. We accepted, but said we wanted to see the place first in case it didn't suit us. He took us to it, and frankly it didn't look suitable. It was more like a bal musette than an up to date cabaret and nightclub. The dance floor was far too large. We said so. How could he change it to our liking? A curtain should be hung in the middle in order to make the floor appear smaller, there should be some spotlights, and those ropes that make you think of a boxing ring should be removed. Furthermore, the spectators should wear ties. Martin agreed to everything except the ties. Le Faisan Doré wasn't in a smart district, and if ties were obligatory many prospective spectators would stay away. We compromised on the spectators in the first three rows to wear ties.

We became pals with Martin who came originally from Marseilles, but had travelled a lot, going to Cairo, then the Middle East, and then to Chicago before ending up in Montreal. Above it all he longed desperately for France. Roche and I were too tactful to ask him why he never returned to France. His friends and associates seemed to be in the same boat as he.

'They look like tough guys,' said Roche after we had met his partners who included Edmond's brother Marius and Vic Cotroni, the latter speaking only English. There were four partners in all; however, we never met the fourth. I am sure Roche would have considered him a tough guy too.

Edmond had kept his word and the transformations we had asked for were ready for our first performance. There were two other performers in our show, namely, Jacques Normand, an awfully pleasant fellow, and Monique Leyrac who resembled a Redskin, and I for one couldn't take my eyes off her. For that opening night the spectators arrived wearing dinner jackets, something Le Faisan Doré had never seen before. Women were in evening dress. I had never seen heavy drinking on such a scale. They drank mostly beer though in enormous quantities. Bottles were replaced the very second they were empty.

Each performance lasted for two hours, and there were two each day, and three on Sunday. It was hard work, and Roche and I both sighed with relief when the date for our departure for New York arrived.

For the second time we had frontier trouble, as if America wasn't too keen to receive us. We had to get off the train because we didn't have work permits. We had to spend a night on the American-Canadian border before we were allowed in.

We remained at the Café Society for five weeks. *J'ai bu* figured in our selection of songs, but now in English. We announced ourselves in English too. While we performed at the Café Society several cabaret directors came to see us to offer contracts. Trying to be clever—probably too clever— we told them we would think it over, and let them know in time, our great idea being the longer we kept them waiting the more they would pay. How wrong we were! When our contract had ended we went to see the gentlemen who had made the offers. None of them wanted us. Thus I learnt that in America you have to accept offers when they are made, and they are usually made while you are still under contract to somebody else—not afterwards.

So there we were broke again. I because I had spent all I had earned, and cautious Roche because his wallet had been stolen in a bar. Mind you, it was a wee bit his own fault. He had put it on the counter, then turned his back on it. The only solution was to go back to Le Faisan Doré in Montreal, a bit of a come-down after the big New York contracts we thought were within reach.

'Come at once,' said Edmond Martin.

He didn't have to say that twice.

Although Roche and I had but one ambition, namely to sing in New York we remained in Montreal for several months. We were doing so well that I asked Micheline, my wife, and Aida, my sister, to join us. They arrived, and Aida got an engagement at the Faisan Doré. However, Micheline soon tired of a life without our daughter Patricia, and returned to Paris.

Shortly afterwards Roche fell madly and seriously in love with a girl called Jocelyne Delongchamps. She was aged sixteen, and was a delightful creature in every sense. On Friday afternoons Roche and I attended auditions in Le Faisan Doré, our aim to discover new talent, and one day Jocelyne appeared at an audition. She sang, moved gracefully and smiled. That smile was the arrow that struck Roche's large heart. A few weeks later he told me he and Jocelyne were engaged to be married. What did I think of it?

'I am all for it,' I said.

He had hardly left the room when my sister Aida came in, looking slightly abashed.

'Charles, can I speak to you?'

'Of course. Anything wrong?'

'Everything's all right.' Then after a brief hesitation. 'I'm getting married.'

And truly enough within forty-eight hours Roche married Jocelyne and Aida, Marcel Diotte who worked with us in Le Faisan Doré.

Roche and I were earning good money, and we had offers for gala performances and we sang on the radio. After all my frustrations and poverty the life of ease went to my head a little. The first move in this life of ease was to buy a car. It was delivered outside the Faisan Doré, and then I was driven to The Tourist Room in it, not because I wanted in my *folie de grandeur* a personal chauffeur: I didn't know how to drive as I had never touched a steering wheel before.

'You're mad,' said Roche, 'to buy such a huge car, and you haven't even got a driving permit.'

'That's my affair.'

Next day I went to get a driving licence. All you had to do at the time in Montreal was to ask for it and pay two dollars and fifty cents when it was handed to you. The official who gave it inquired whether I was accustomed to driving cars.

'That's all I've been doing in Paris these last ten years,' was my answer.

I got into the car and drove off. The first tram that saw me ran straight into the car. It had the cheek to drag the car along for a while which left the car in a poor state. Never mind, cars are made to be repaired. And repaired it was. At my next sortie it skidded off the road and hit a snow bank. That couldn't have happened in a warm climate, so it wasn't really my fault.

When I bought the car nobody had told me that cars need oil. I had to discover that all on my own, and when I did it was too late.

'This car is dead,' said the garagekeeper whom I called in.

Luckily friends who were in the motor trade lent me a car. I couldn't live without a car any more. I drove that car till they telephoned to tell me I should bring it back because they had sold it. They did, however, lend me another. But that wasn't enough. I needed a car of my own. I bought one which I sold at a loss to buy a faster one, which I sold at a loss too to buy an even faster one, and so it went. When Parisian friends of mine turned up in Montreal and saw me in my latest car they took me for a millionaire, and I found that most gratifying.

I also threw myself into male elegance. I had a new suit made every week, at fifty dollars a suit. When Roche decided to return to Paris to introduce his young wife to his parents he asked me to accompany them. My suits filled several trunks. We took passage on a French liner, and when I saw my suits hanging in the wardrobe of my stateroom I couldn't help saying to myself that my friends and relations would admire me open mouthed. I smiled broadly at the thought of it.

However, the smile went when I entered Piaf's drawing room in Paris, wearing an almond green suit and a wide tie with an American bathing beauty on it.

'What's this?' she said. 'Are you working in a circus now?'

'This is a suit I bought in Canada, and it's made to measure.'

'You take yourself for a woman,' she shouted. 'Change into something else at once. What else have you got?'

'A pale blue suit, a rose coloured suit, a silver-grey suit, a yellow Prince of Wales suit . . .'

'Got a lot of all that?'

'Five trunkfuls.'

'Throw the lot away. Not even a rag and bone man would buy them. Anyhow, in my presence you won't wear any of them.'

'Do you want me to walk round naked?'

She said that would be preferable, and I went home to my parents, where I changed into an old, black velvet suit, then I returned to Piaf.

'It suits you far better,' she said. 'Anyhow, you wore black when I met you. Now that you begin to look like a man again, tell me about your plans.'

I told her that Roche and I planned to have some well paid gala performances in Paris before returning to Canada.

'Why well paid?' asked Piaf.

'We were a great success in Montreal.'

'So you think the clock has stopped because a couple of tramps called Roche and Aznavour were successful in a country that has no artistic sense whatever. And do you really think they're waiting for you in Paris? Poor idiot. They've forgotten you long ago.'

I didn't say anything. With her one had to wait for her anger to subside. Like waiting for the sea to calm. But my silence didn't stop her.

'Who gave you the stupid idea of going back to Canada? A Frenchman can make his career as an artiste only in France. So kindly forget all your nonsense, and remain in France.'

She wasn't speaking to deaf ears. Roche, of course, had every right and reason to return to Canada since his wife was Canadian, and it had been their intention from the start to make their home there. As we had been partners and close friends for many years it had seemed logical to continue throwing in my lot with him. When I say it seemed logical I mean it had seemed so before we left Canada, but once back in Paris I realised without admitting to myself that Canada was a small country indeed. If France was small then Canada was ten times smaller. It needed Piaf to bring that to the surface. I am the first to admit that she had a lasting influence on me from the very start. Hadn't it been she who had sent me to America in the first instance?

Yet it was a heartbreaking thought to dissolve the partnership of Roche and Aznavour.

However, breaking up the partnership wasn't enough for Piaf. She wanted to break up something else too, which was almost easier because it was breaking up on its own.

'You're going to move in here,' continued Piaf. 'I nearly forgot you're married. What will your wife say?'

'Not much,' I said.

For the fact was that my marriage with Micheline was nearing its end. I had felt that while she was in Montreal, and felt it even more when she decided to go back to Paris. Since my return to Paris I heard the word divorce daily, and daily too she enumerated her wrongs which admittedly had a basis. I preferred my work to my wife whom I neglected. My friends meant more to me than my wife. I preferred playing the piano to going out with her. I never whispered words of love to her, whereas I wrote such excellent songs about love. I didn't take her with me on my travels, and so on and so forth. Of course she didn't forget to tell me that she had given me the best years of her life.

When I got tired of listening to her I agreed to the divorce, and moved in with Piaf. I left Patricia with my parents.

In my profession Piaf was a miracle, a permanent miracle. You don't resist a miracle. I for one didn't.

The break with Roche was even more painful. I knew Piaf was right in saying we should part, and Charles Trenet had said roughly the same. Two singers could never make a career together. One has to be on one's own to have a name. Trenet understood my feelings. 'I know what you feel,' he said. 'When you leave a partner it's like leaving a mistress.'

I appreciated the reasons that forced Roche to go back to Canada, where his wife's family lived, and where an excellent situation awaited him. He had chosen security while I chose insecurity as living with Piaf offered no security whatever. She took a great affection for a person only to drop him when the affection shifted to someone else. She could forget one in twenty-four hours. Then perhaps she remembered the person after a year. In short, she was no exception to the rule where friendship is concerned, but that didn't give one any sense of security in her admirable presence.

She was nine years older than I, consequently most of the people round her were much older than I. They—the surviving ones—are in their seventies today. Being the youngest in her setup only added to my sense of insecurity.

I explained all that to Roche who was most understanding. 'You can't sing a duet with one in Montreal the other in Paris.'

'You're perfectly right,' said Roche.

But to break an eight-year-old friendship and partnership is no easy matter. We sang together for the last time at a gala performance. Then we walked away together as we had done thousands of times.

'Good luck, Charles.'

'Good luck, Pierre.'

Our roads parted. I went to live in Piaf's house.

It was almost unfurnished, and I was put into a room with flying buttresses, and there I remained. I became a sort of chauffeur-secretary, but also an accomplice with whom she could laugh and drink neck to neck. And of course I answered the telephone.

When I sang in public I felt like an orphan, and had the impression that a second voice was missing in my throat—Roche's. My voice sounded sadly lonely to me. Even the best pianist couldn't give me the moral backing Roche's piano playing gave. Edith Piaf encouraged me, yet I remained depressed.

In the daytime I was usually in Raoul Breton's office; in the evenings I was with Piaf; at night I dragged myself from one Montmartre nightclub to another in the company of Florence Véran, Richard Marsan and Jean-Louis Marquet, old friends I hadn't seen since before my Canadian days. I got drunk steadily, I drank as if drinking were a duty.

'A man who doesn't know himself,' I observed between two hiccups, 'will never get anywhere in life. Qualities don't count. To get on one must use one's shortcomings to one's advantage.'

I was deeply moved by my profound thoughts, and when I got into bed at dawn I meditated on what I had said. Suddenly I rose, sat down at a table, and put to paper the fruit of my meditation. That sheet of paper is still in my possession.

'My shortcomings are my voice, my height, my gestures, my lack of culture and education, my frankness and my lack of personality.'

Fair enough, so I wrote on.

'Nothing can be done about my voice. The experts I have spoken to were all categorical about it. Their advice was I should stop singing. But I'll go on singing as long as I live. With a little effort I can reach three octaves. My possibilities can become as good as any classical singer's despite the fog that covers the timbre of my voice.

'My height: I am one metre sixty-four centimetres, but nothing can be done about that. My only attempt to find a solution had ended in disaster. In New York I had worn "elevator-shoes", and people thought I had two clubfeet. The only answer is to accept my height while persuading others to forget it.

'My gestures: they are the gestures of small people, far too brusque. I must change that, and move less jerkily. If I go through a door that is higher than one metre and seventy centimetres I will stoop like people who are much taller than I. Perhaps that will rid me of my complex.

'My lack of culture: I had the biggest difficulty getting my school certificate. I learn nothing on my own, and I learn only when listening to others.

'My frankness: I am incorrigible. I shout if I sense injustice, and I say *merde* to anybody however important he is when I feel like it.

'My lack of personality: to get myself noticed despite my lack of height I dress in an eccentric fashion. People do notice me but with a smile.

'I who had been a timid child must turn myself into a strong personality without losing the moral principles I learnt from my parents, that is listen to my heart, remain tender and capable of tears.

'I must build up myself to be able to realise myself. I must refuse to accept the present but turn towards the future. Yet not disown the past. The French chanson is my foundation stone, also the folklore of the world and the poetry of the Orient, especially Armenian poetry.'

I re-read what I had written, agreed with it, and swore I would act and behave accordingly. Then I lay down and slept the sleep of the just and the drunk.

One morning in 1950 Piaf appeared in the kitchen, wearing an old dressing gown that was nearly in shreds. I was drinking tea and eating bread and butter. The cook was cleaning vegetables. Piaf took a cup and poured herself tea.

'We're off to New York in a few days,' she announced. 'You, Charles, I'm taking with me. You'll look after the stage lighting and do odd jobs. In short, you'll make yourself useful. And watching me you'll learn your profession.'

She drank her tea, then said that now that we were leaving Paris in a short while we ought to go out every night. As if we had ever stayed indoors!

When Piaf went out she went to town in every sense, there were no half measures with her. Whatever she did she had to do it thoroughly and completely till she tired of it. The same applied to food and everything else that awakened her interest of the moment. If she decided she loved eating steak tartare, she ate steak tartare at every meal. That would last a whole month. Escalope à la crème followed the steak tartare, and it lasted even longer. I couldn't touch escalope à la crème for years after my surfeit of that diet. If you wanted to eat something else she observed, 'Naturally you want something else because you have no sensibility.' The only answer was to eat the same whether you were tired of it or not.

When Gilbert Bécaud entered our circle he didn't know how to treat Piaf and how to react to her, whereas I had become accustomed to her peculiar ways ever since we lived under the same roof. We went out to dinner with Bécaud and three other people. She said to the headwaiter, 'Give me chicken. What about you?'

'Chicken,' I said.

'Chicken,' said the other three.

'Six chicken,' said Piaf to the headwaiter.

'I'll have sausage,' said Bécaud.

I kicked him under the table.

'Not chicken?' said Piaf, raising her eyebrows.

'No, I'll have sausage,' said Bécaud, not heeding my kick.

From that moment onward Piaf hated him, and nobody succeeded in stopping that hatred.

She was truly unbelievable. We went one night, she and I, to a first night of Yves Montand just before our departure to America. 'You will see how wonderful he is,' she said when we sat down. 'Wonderful and marvellous, simply fantastic.'

Montand was all that and even more. After the show, she went to congratulate him, but later that evening I found her waiting for me at L'Elysée Matignan, our café, with her arms folded and a furious expression on her face. 'The swine,' she spat, 'he's pinched everything he sings from me.'

Not a word of it was true. There was absolutely nothing in his singing or his repertoire of songs that could in any way remind one of Piaf. She had made that odious remark because it reassured her. She was made like that.

This story has a sequel later on in my life, when I had become successful and she came to hear me sing. She came backstage and said all the things: 'You were the greatest,' and 'Your show is beautiful' and 'I cried in the audience.' Later, I arrived at our favourite café, the Elysée Matignan, which we had re-christened L'Elysée M'As Tu Va? to find Piaf surrounded by her côterie. At first, I refused to sit down. 'Any minute now,' I told her, 'you will tell me that I am a swine, and I pinched everything from you.' How she laughed. It is that enormous laugh coming from that frail little body which most moves me in the memory of Edith. It is her laugh I miss most.

One day she asked one of us which was the best film at the moment. *The Third Man*, one of us unluckily said. We all went with her to see the film. She found it marvellous, wonderful and fantastic too. She took us to see that film every night for a whole endless week. I never got so sick and tired of any film in my life.

She had periods of classical music. During those periods one had to stay in and listen respectfully to classical records. There were periods of literature too, and she would explain to us in her fashion what Marcel Proust or Teilhard de Chardin meant in their books.

Such was the woman who was taking me to America as her 'lighting man'.

Being somewhat broke at the time Piaf sold her luxurious car to be able to pay for the tickets to New York. Once in New York she took a suite in a hotel on the twenty-third floor in 50th Street near the cabaret called Versailles. I had a tiny room on the third floor. The view from my window was a wall that was so near that if I stretched out my arm I could touch it. Piaf decided to go to the cinema on the evening of our arrival. She looked at the cinema programme in a newspaper, then she shouted, 'Children, we're in luck. *The Third Man* is still on in a little cinema. Charles, get us a taxi.'

In the cinema I sat ten rows behind her, my excuse being that my eyes were tired. I fell asleep the moment the film began. I was brutally awakened by someone shaking me. It was Piaf.

'So you're sleeping,' she said accusingly. 'I pay you the signal honour of bringing you here to see a masterpiece, and all you do is to snore.'

I tried to excuse myself, saying it was the voyage and the difference in hours that had tired me out. It wasn't good enough, and she told me she would punish me by not taking me again to see *The Third Man*.

The other members of our circle envied me the punishment.

'As you're so tired you'll go straight to bed,' she said when we got back to the hotel. 'The rest of us will drink champagne in my suite.'

She didn't have to tell me twice. 'Have a good time,' I said, and rushed to my tiny room, where I jumped into bed and fell asleep.

The telephone bell yanked me out of my profound slumber in the middle of the night.

'Come up at once,' said Piaf's voice.

I took the lift to her suite still half asleep.

'I don't know what's happening,' she said, 'but living on the twenty-third floor doesn't suit me at all, and I'm sure that the top of the house is swaying.'

'What do you intend to do about it?'

'I'm going to move.'

'Move where?'

'You take the suite, and I go down to your room.'

Nothing surprising about that because she had done that before. Her bedroom in her house in Boulogne-sur-Seine had been decorated and furnished in the best Marie-Antoinette manner. The very night she had moved into the bedroom she woke me up to tell me she was going to sleep in my little hole as she didn't feel at ease in her bedroom. With Piaf history, that is her history, often repeated itself. But on that night in New York she surpassed herself. She wished to take all her luggage down to my tiny room at once.

At that late hour there was no hotel staff, so I had to take up my belongings first, then carry hers down. The lift went continuously up and down while the move took place. At last it was over, I lay down, fell back into sleep only to be wakened by the telephone again.

'Come down,' she commanded.

I found her standing in her nightdress in the middle of the tiny room. She was in a very bad mood.

'It sways here too,' she said. 'The whole district is swaying, I think.'

'What will you do about it?'

'I'm going back to the suite.'

It's the champagne that makes New York sway, I said to myself while I attended to the luggage.

She drank heavily during the American tour. When she sang at the Versailles she frequently complained of having blackouts. Those of us who were close to her knew perfectly the cause of the blackouts, namely the bottle, yet the audiences never noticed it.

She took us on a free night to see a play in which John Garfield acted. She fell for him in a big way. To repay the courtesy he came to the Versailles to hear her sing. When she returned to the hotel she found him in the nude in her bedroom, waiting for her. She told us she had sent him packing, but that was a lie. He stayed the night with her.

94

The next night she went to the theatre to see Garfield again, and she repeated that on many other nights. As she had two performances a day she just managed to get to the theatre for a few minutes, naturally always at the same time, and on each occasion she repeated, 'Isn't he marvellous.'

It was almost a repetition of *The Third Man*.

Chapter Eight

Slowly I began to understand what Piaf had meant when she said before our departure that accompanying her I would learn a lot about my profession. To start with I met a lot of important people through her. They came to congratulate her after performances, and among them were Charlie Chaplin, Judy Garland, Ginger Rogers and all the other Hollywood stars. Piaf knew how to draw people to her. She was like a magnet. Those famous people got to know me too thanks to her. Thus when years later I came to America on my own I didn't come as an unknown person. Mind you, that had its drawbacks too.

The Versailles, where Piaf sang in New York, was run by a man of Greek origin. When the time came for me to start on my first American tour my agent approached him, suggesting he engage a young singer who was already well known in France and who had immense potential. The Greek told him to send the publicity stuff, and when he saw my photograph he recognised me.

'Honest, I can't engage Miss Piaf's light man.'

So I never sang in the Versailles.

Living in Piaf's company had many advantages however. It wasn't a matter of her influencing me. Her influence was neither bad nor good because there was no influence. Many have said that Piaf influenced young artistes. It was even said that she made them. Anyhow, in my case there was none of that. Ours was deep friendship and complicity, especially complicity. She left the lighting entirely to me. When I said I would do so and so she answered, 'Do whatever you want as long as you light up the fingers of my right hand.'

I learnt a lot watching her at work. After all, if you see a person of great talent at work as often as I saw Piaf—and I mean for years and years—it is inevitable that one learns a great deal from them. I learned how one has to work to achieve success, yet, strangely enough, we never discussed the chanson as such. Piaf didn't explain the tricks of her trade—if that is the right expression. I think the reason she was unable to explain them was that everything was purely instinctive with her. But she did harness her instincts to her talent. She would make an instinctive gesture that gave the chanson its whole strength. She herself didn't know and couldn't explain why she had made that gesture. Once she had made it and saw how successful it was she repeated it every time she sang that song. Or she didn't if she found an even more impressive gesture. Yes, with Piaf everything was a matter of instinct.

There are artistes who spend hours in front of the mirror trying out gestures. I never saw Piaf doing that, yet the spectators cried out with pleasure, 'What wonderful gestures!' And they went away convinced that it had taken her months to think them up. Thus I learnt from her the art of being spontaneous on the stage.

I always loved my audiences, and Piaf loved hers too though she was frightened by crowds, whereas they don't frighten me. If autograph hunters came to her she nearly panicked. It wasn't reluctance to give autographs: it was sheer fright.

When she and I discussed songs we talked only of the lyrics, that is whether they were good or bad, but we didn't discuss how they should be sung, which is as it should be because our profession is based more on the chanson than on singing it. The Americans look at songs as part of a show. It isn't so with us. We sing one song, then another song, then a third song, but it isn't a show: just so many songs, each on its own. The Americans don't gesture while they sing: Piaf and later I found our gestures while singing on the stage.

The singer (according to our ideas and principles) has to make gestures for the audience to realise that there isn't only the song but the singer too. Often his presence means more to the audience than the quality of the song. Naturally, the singer needs a very special gift to achieve that. Piaf had it, Yves Montand has it, though his gestures are far more elaborate. However, the idea is the same, namely not to remain on the stage without doing something, be it a gesture or a look. It is difficult to lay down rules or give a precise explanation. An actor can explain how he puts on a hat, but there is nothing of the kind in our profession which is definitely a more simple one. Piaf was a very simple singer. She appeared on stage wearing her simple little dress, and created her magic like that.

Now let us go back to the light man on Piaf's American tour.

While Piaf sang at the Versailles she discovered a new vocation: she would be a painter. She painted lying on her bed. She painted members of her entourage, and they had to sit on the bed while acting as models. I wasn't included. 'You're too stupid for it,' she said.

'I'm not stupid, I just haven't got the patience,' said I.

'Painting is a serious matter,' she said, then shouted at the unfortunate model because he didn't sit still.

When the painting was finished she told me to look at it. 'Well?' she asked.

'There certainly is a resemblance,' I said.

'A resemblance? It's him.'

'If you say so.'

'It isn't if I say so,' she shouted. 'It's him, and if you can't see it it's because there's shit in your eyes.'

As a matter of fact her paintings were so naive that even a child of six would have found them too crude.

Ironically enough she had a bosom friend in New York, a Frenchwoman called Reine, who ran an art gallery. She came to Piaf's dressing room to see her, and while she was there she suddenly noticed me, my long nose probably reminding her of her origins. She first asked Piaf who I was. 'A young man who follows me everywhere,' was the reply. Then Reine turned to me and inquired whether I was a Jew.

'Not that I know of,' I said.

'Nevertheless, you have an awful nose.'

'It's mine.'

'I never thought you had pinched it from somebody else. It's so big that he would have noticed and missed it.'

In the course of our pleasant chat she suggested I should have my nose shortened. 'They do it so well here. Edith, don't you agree?'

'I've got accustomed to it,' said Piaf.

Reine went on harping on my nose, repeating I should have it shortened. What did I intend to do in life? Sing. One added reason for the operation.

Eddy Constantine was Piaf's great love by then. I dined with them after the performance, and she brought up my nose again, remarking that there was something in what Reine had said. I protested, saying I was born with that nose and it hadn't done me any harm yet. Lou Levy was also at our table, and he said that now that everybody in New York believed that I was a Jew I hadn't any excuse left to say no to the operation. He knew an excellent surgeon who specialised in noses, and he would attend to mine for a song. Before I could open my mouth Piaf asked him to telephone the surgeon whose name was Irwing Goldman. 'And fix an appointment for Charles.'

Thus I fell into the trap.

Against my better judgment I went to see the surgeon who showed me photographs of famous people—before and after. He made me a sketch of my future profile. It didn't look bad at all. Goldman booked me a room in a nursing home, Lou paid for it, in short it was Piaf who offered me my new nose. I would be operated on in a week's time.

On the night before the operation Piaf took me to a French Restaurant called Le Pavillon to celebrate the demise of my long nose. Naturally, champagne was ordered.

'But I mustn't take anything before the operation,' I protested. 'The surgeon said so.'

'He meant food, not drink,' said Piaf.

Though I wasn't too sure of that I agreed with her because I did want to drink champagne. By six in the morning we were all pretty drunk.

'I wonder whether we didn't make a mistake,' said Piaf all of a sudden.

'I'm entering the nursing home in an hour's time,' I bleated.

'I'm not joking,' said Piaf. 'I'm honestly afraid that we'll regret it afterwards. A shorter nose might take away your personality.'

'It's all fixed,' I said. 'Goldman is expecting me, he's been paid in advance, so I can't back out.'

'Fundamentally it's your affair,' she said treacherously. 'If you find yourself with the head of a monster you can only blame yourself.'

After the operation I went to see her and Eddy Constantine with a bandage on my nose.

'My poor Charles,' she said. 'What a terrible sight, the state you must be in.'

When I flew back to Paris my nose was still bandaged. Piaf would follow later as her contract hadn't expired yet. My main reason for going back earlier was a stupid quarrel we had had. I can't even remember what it was about. Our brushes were always insignificant and unnecessary, yet we took them dead seriously at the time. We would have a row over a play we had seen. I liked it, she didn't, and she would shout, 'You know nothing about plays. If you like such a play you're not worthy of living with us.' Or something even more trivial. When we had this particular set-to, I said. 'Pay my ticket, I'm going back.'

And back to Paris I travelled.

The liner had hardly left its moorings when I received a cable from her. 'Imbecile, why have you left?' Such was Piaf.

When it was her turn to leave New York she cabled to ask me to meet her at the airport.

There was a number of us waiting for her at the airport. She kissed and embraced everybody who had come to meet her, but ignored me. I smiled at her, I grinned, I stood close to her, nothing doing, she continued to ignore me. Of course, I was indignant and deeply hurt. Her friends went in search of their cars to race to her house in Boulogne-sur-Seine to celebrate her return. I, who just couldn't understand why she was cutting me dead, went to her car with her chauffeur, and waited for her because I had to find out what was the matter.

'Edith?' I said when she appeared.

'But it's you!' she exclaimed in a surprised voice.

'Who else did you think I was?'

'This is terribly funny. I do recognise your voice. I was furious with you, saying to myself the swine hasn't turned up, he's surely with some girl.'

'I was at the airport before anybody else, yet every time I approached you you turned your back on me.'

'I didn't recognise you,' she laughed. 'I was in fact wondering who that cunt was who was trying to get near me all the time.'

When we arrived in Boulogne-sur-Seine all her friends were in the house, waiting to celebrate her return, among them Eddy Constantine who had been with us in New York (as I have mentioned.)

It was I who had introduced him to her some time after Cerdan's death in an air crash in the Azores in 1949. His death had upset Piaf terribly, she wore mourning for him and cut her hair short. I was in Canada at the time, and when I came back she telephoned me. 'Come, I'm all alone.' I arrived, and it was like going into a crypt. Everything was in darkness, and really and truly she was all alone. In the evening I suggested we go out. She refused to come with me as suffering alone was part and parcel of her mourning. Nevertheless I did go out, and in fact took her car which she didn't need. In those days in France there was a plaque with the owner's name on the windscreen of every car. People read the name, and said, 'Ah, Piaf,' which was of immense help to me when I went in search of work in it.

On that night I was only too glad to drive away from her house. Ours had been a painful evening because I had to be extremely careful not to mention Cerdan or any place she had been with him. It would have caused a frightening scene if I had reminded her in any way of the man whose loss filled her thoughts and heart. I took myself to a restaurant called Chez Carrère which was well known at the time. It had an orchestra, and a male American and an American woman sang with it. The woman was called Maryleen, and I fancied her very much. She introduced me to the male American who was none other than Eddy Constantine. We got on extremely well, and I thought here was the right man to yank Piaf out of her sadness.

I said to her some days later, 'Edith, I want you to meet a young man I know.'

'I don't want to know any young man. You're mad to suggest it.'

'I'm certain you'll need him for your next American tour. I insist on introducing him. He has translated some of your chansons.'

I had prepared Constantine for the meeting, and when we went together to Piaf I said before we entered her presence, 'Smile as you smiled at me on the night we met. You'll see how well she'll get on with you.'

I went in to announce him, and she said. 'Some other time,' but I insisted again, reminding her that she was leaving soon for America and she needed chansons. The young American could help. There was a large mirror in the room, and in the mirror she could see the waiting Constantine. 'Hi,' he said, turning towards her, and that was the second death of Cerdan. Nonetheless, she never forgot him. She went every week to Mass with Constantine to pray for Cerdan's soul. But it was definitely her meeting Constantine that brought back her lust for life. Their affair lasted for about two years which was the usual time for one of her grand passions to run. When the rise began so to speak she wore hats, a lot of make-up, and dressed with care. Once the man fell into the trap there was no more make-up but only foundation cream, and she forgot about hats although she possessed many that she hardly ever wore. The same went for her dresses. She had at least fifteen black dresses, but she always wore the same one.

Her years with Constantine were one of the best periods of her life in every sense. Firstly he was extremely kind to her, secondly he was always present when she needed him. She slept little during the day, seldom at night. Constantine did the same to please her. When they went to a show or the cinema he sat behind her to be able to catch up on his sleep a little. Suddenly she would turn back. 'Eddie, isn't that so?'

'Of course, it is.'

He gave her good advice, and he wasn't a man who thought only of success. Naturally, he wanted to get on but not at any price. She was terribly proud of him. During this period she had a very innocent Breton maid whom she loved to shock and one day when she was in bed with Eddie Constantine, the maid came into the bedroom and Edith threw off the covers and said, 'Did you ever see anything like that?'

'Oh, madame,' shrieked the maid.

While she loved him she followed the same procedure as with all her other lovers.

She was always very fussy about what her lovers wore, and always insisted, by degrees, that they went to her tailor and chose what she liked, even when they had been well-dressed before. This dominance began nicely with a present from Edith of some gold cuff-links from Boucheron, then followed the cigarette holder lovingly inscribed. We always knew the progress of a love affair when first the cuff-links, then the cigarette holder appeared.

After that, she sent them to the tailor and they would emerge soberly suited in blue with which they had to wear a white or pale blue shirt and a reticently striped tie. She liked her lovers to look like gentlemen. Once, one of them had the temerity to decide on his own tailor and his departure from the norm caused quite an outrage. There were very funny scenes sometimes when a new lover had just reached the blue suit stage and one or two old flames would call round, identically dressed.

It is easy to see why Edith was so appalled by my colourful Canadian clothes, and made me change into my old black velvet suit. Even Ted Lapidus refused to make me coloured suits in those days. He said it would ruin his reputation. In the end he agreed to make coloured jeans, as a concession to me. In those days in Paris there was a great feeling for black and sober colours in dress. Juliette Greco and the existentialists dressed only in black and the Left Bank looked a very drab place. In fact, the life and language were very colourful indeed, especially Edith's.

The climate around Edith was always vivid. She'd think nothing of demanding pickled herrings at three o'clock in the morning when we were both drunk and we'd get in the car, and I'd drive like crazy all over Paris on a wild goose chase to satisfy her sudden craving for pickled herrings.

We had a lot of fun, but most of all, we had complicity and an extraordinary level of communication, which came from having the same hard background in the streets and the bals musettes, and singing with an accordion, for money. With one eye moving, we knew if the other needed to laugh or cry or work; whether they needed warmth or toughness.

Piaf used to call me her *genie-con* (genius cunt) and it was more in affection than in mockery. She believed in me as a young lyric writer and composer. She was always asking me to play jazzy things, new things on the piano, saying 'Stop,' knowing my opinion almost before I did. When I was away, she used to call me to tell me she was in love. Of course, I was in love with her too, from the first week I met her. Everyone always was, she had such extraordinary talent. She knew, of course, that she was not Marilyn Monroe. She was small, she didn't have a beautiful body, she didn't have a lovely face: she was no Ava Gardner. But with Piaf, one by one, everything was beautiful, her nose elegant, her eyes beautiful, and she was lovely on stage when she sang.

Of course, for Piaf, the first week when I was 'in-love' with her was a lifetime, and I think, she felt throughout our association that I still loved her and that one day we would have an affair. She thought I kept my feelings hidden and I let her believe it because she needed to feel loved. Sometimes when we were very drunk she would lie all over me and kiss me and say, 'Don't worry, we'll end up together, that's for sure.' Then we'd go out and I'd meet someone and she'd arrange it for me, and so it continued.

She was in many ways like a spider, and one felt trapped by her. Women, especially, were afraid of her, afraid of being trapped, except for her great friend Marlene Dietrich, to whom she looked up. And also Lena Horne.

When Piaf felt on top, she talked non-stop, but when she gave someone advice, she would say, 'This is when one shuts one's trap and one listens.' And she could listen, enraptured, like a bobby-soxer. 'The greatest ability for people like us', she would say to me, 'is to listen when we meet people who know more.'

Despite our close friendship, deep mutual understanding and rare complicity I decided to leave Piaf's house after one of our American tours. Raoul Breton, my music publisher, had said to me on our return, 'If you continue in Piaf's shadow you'll never make a career. Your duty to yourself is to cut yourself loose from her. She has done a lot for you, nonetheless you must leave her. Give me your word that you'll move out of her house for one year at least.'

I gave my word, and when I give it I keep it.

Piaf understood my motives. She was the first to admit that she was in the way of any success that might come my way. She did regret my decision because she was a fundamentally lonely woman, and above everything else we laughed a lot together. I knew how to make her laugh, and I enjoyed hearing her laugh.

So I moved out of the house, and into an apartment in the rue Villaret-de-Joyeuse in the 17th arrondissement, where my old friends Florence Véran, Richard Marsan and Billy Florent lived. The rent was pretty stiff, and frequently we weren't able to pay it. The proprietor came from time to time to try to collect the rent. Nobody opened the door.

'Open the door,' he shouted. 'I know you're in.'

We held our breath.

'If you don't pay I'll have you thrown out by the police.'

We didn't open the door, and he, to revenge himself, cut off the central heating and the hot water. Drink and blankets saved us on cold days.

Richard and Florence were a loving, tormented couple. She wrote songs, and he imitated the famous such as Raimu, Jouvet, Jules Berry and Jean Tissier. Now and again I worked with Florence which consisted of my shouting the lyrics while she banged the piano.

Notwithstanding our hand to mouth existence Richard and I each had a car, and we drove at night in them either to Saint-Germain-des-Prés or to the Butte-Montmartre. Our favourite drink was red table wine, and we insisted on it even in the most fashionable night clubs. From time to time we took our children for a walk. I fetched Patricia from my parents, and with Florence's daughter Marianne we drove into the country.

Florence, Richard and I often went late at night up to the Butte in the company of Jean-Louis Marquet who had taken my place in Piaf's household. We went either to Pomme or to Geneviève, and apart from music and red wine finding a girl for the night was my aim. I rarely failed.

In the mornings I never got up late, and went out to find impresarios to engage me to sing for paltry sums. However Bohemian a life one leads one can't exist without a few sous in one's pocket. In the afternoons I went usually to Raoul Breton who was my mainstay and pillar of strength in those lean times. He morally helped me to accept my lack of luck. He believed in me, and in his office I tried hard to sell my chansons to more successful artistes.

One afternoon he informed me that he had fixed a date for me with Patachou, his erstwhile secretary, who had made her fame in her cabaret-restaurant by cutting with scissors the

Above: Singing with Tom Jones
Below: Singing with Liza Minnelli during his American TV special

To Charles —
the Man who has
everything —

Love
Ryan

1969

Above: Charles—'the man who has everything'—with Ryan O'Neal while making the fi
The Games, 1969
Below: The Games

Above: Charles, Hardy Kruger and Lino Ventura in *Un Taxi Pour Tobruk*, 1961
Below: Charles and James Coburn filming *The Sky Riders*

Above: Charles and Frank Sinatra in Las Vegas
Below: In St Tropez with Virna Lisi during the filming of *Le Temps des Loups*

GERARD LEROUX

J. ANDANSON/SYGMA

Above: Charles and Maurice Chevalier crowning each other
Below: Charles, Bruno Coquatrix and Liza Minnelli in Paris, December 1978

Above left: Charles with his children Katia and Misha and their dog
Above right: Charles with his son Nicholas
Below: With his wife, Ulla

Left: With Ursula Andress
Right: With Raquel Welch during her only French TV show, *Aznavour Special*
Below: Charles singing in the open air arena in Verona to an audience of 30,000

Above: Charles with his favourite writing partner and brother-in-law, George Garvaren
Below: Charles, shaking hands with HRH Queen Elizabeth at a Royal Comman
Performance, 1975

customers' ties. They evidently liked that. Chez Patachou in the rue Mont-Cenis on the Butte-Montmarte was simply crowded every night. She used to come regularly to Breton's office in the afternoons, not only because they had remained friends but because she sang several songs by Trenet whose publisher was Breton. Breton was fond of her, and being fond of me too it was natural that he should mention me to her.

Here I must go back in time a little. There was a Jewish singer called Leo Fuld who had been an enormous success in the United States in the years 1947–48. He came to France, and his fame grew as much as in America. He sang in English and in French. He had starred with Piaf at the ABC, which was a great event. He was looking for new songs, that is for songs in a new style. When one spoke of the new style my name was invariably mentioned. He was advised to meet me, and that was why we met. I was generally very timid when I presented my chansons. In Breton's office I used to wear dark glasses because they gave me the feeling that I could hide behind them. Fuld was impressed by my songs, said they were excellent indeed, and I should sing them in public.

'But I sing them in public,' I said.

'Where?'

'At the Crazy Horse Saloon, where I sing every night.'

He came to see me at the Crazy Horse Saloon. 'Your performance is very bad,' he said. 'If you want to become a star you must make women feel that you need consolation. You must look ill and emaciated. You must become like Sinatra, as if one couldn't see you behind the mike.'

I listened to him, and worked that line. Patachou arrived in my life after my meeting with Fuld.

Her husband had been a pastry-cook, hence the nickname Patachou, but it was her husband who made the pastry, not she. The pastry-shop became the cabaret-restaurant called Chez Patachou. In Breton's office she heard me sing my chansons while I accompanied myself on the piano. Breton had left us alone after introducing us to each other.

'Are you shortsighted?' Patachou asked.

'No, madame.'

'Then why do you wear those glasses?'

'Because my eyes are tired,' I said, loth to admit my fear which was the same thing as stage fright.

But then, as always happens to me, I forgot her presence, and sang and played only for myself. My voice was rather hoarse at the time. When I had stopped she said she liked my work a great deal, and said she was ready to engage me to sing Chez Patachou.

'You at the piano with your dark glasses,' she said, 'and the light focussed on you could be very impressive.'

'I don't wear glasses when I sing in public.'

'Then don't wear glasses.'

'I don't want to accompany myself,' I said, 'I play the piano too badly, and I don't play in the same key I sing in.'

'Then what do you want?'

'To be accompanied on the piano while I sing standing up in front of the mike.'

'Agreed. Come and see me when you've shaken your cold off.'

'But I haven't a cold. This is my normal voice.'

'Do you smoke a lot?'

'Three packets a day.'

'You drink too?'

'A fair amount.'

'Listen to me now. You'll do me the favour of not smoking for three weeks, which is plenty of time for your voice to become normal again. At the end of the three weeks come up to the Butte, and you can start at once.'

I stopped smoking and went to see her when the three weeks were up. My voice was even hoarser.

'I asked you not to smoke,' she said.

'I didn't smoke for three weeks.'

She shook her head, sighed and said, 'Go and buy a packet of cigarettes, smoke like a chimney, and come back the moment you feel your voice is normal again.'

My first appearance Chez Patachou was a real triumph. All my friends were present, Piaf included. Chevalier had come too, and complimented me in warm tones. Chevalier loved giving advice. 'Don't sing this one but that one,' and so on. It was usually sound advice, but he went on with it for too long.

Piaf wasn't far behind him. I should give my chansons to others for them to sing, and I should sing their chansons.

'Out of the question,' I said.

'Out of the question? Don't be so pretentious.'

'It isn't being pretentious. I write my own songs, and it's logical for me to sing them. It's the only way for me to get anywhere.'

'I'm leaving shortly for Marseilles. If you do as I tell you I'm willing to take you along with me. If not, you can stay and rot in Paris.'

'Bon voyage,' I said.

So once again we had fallen out.

After Patachou I went to Canada for four weeks, which was a disappointment. They missed the old partnership of Roche and Aznavour. Despite that I was offered an extension of my contract. But then I received a cable from Piaf. 'I can't get married without your presence. Come back at once.' There was no extension of contract because, of course, I packed immediately and returned to Paris.

It was noon when I entered Piaf's drawing room, perfectly aware that she would still be sleeping. A young man sat in an armchair, and naturally I imagined that here was the future bridegroom. We introduced ourselves. His name was Gilbert Bécaud, and he told me that he accompanied Jacques Pills on the piano.

'Tell me how it happened,' I said.

'Rather stupidly. We came to show her a chanson we'd specially written for her.'

I examined his features carefully, saying to myself that he certainly had a devilish talent to make Piaf's conquest in such a short time.

Suddenly Jacques Pills appeared, coming straight from her bedroom. He was wearing a dressing gown, and he said in a voice full of tenderness, 'She has just opened her eyes.' His smile made me see my error. It wasn't Bécaud but Pills who was the future husband.

'I'll take her breakfast in,' said Pills.

When we were alone again Bécaud and I chatted about chansons. He sat down at the piano and played for me, and I realised that here was somebody who would go a long way in our profession.

Piaf arrived with Pills in her old dressing-gown. We embraced. As I have said, anger or rancour never lasted with us.

'I've been thinking,' she said. 'I agree with you. You must sing your own songs. We're going on a tour, Jacques, you and I. Bécaud and you will write songs for Jacques, something fresh, young and out of the ordinary.'

And I went on tour with them. We travelled in two cars, Piaf, Pills and Bécaud in the first, I with the luggage in the second. Kiki, Bécaud's fiancée, was also in the second car because Piaf didn't want any woman in hers.

I was back in Piaf's orbit. Had I ever left it?

Chapter Nine

We were in the town of Royat. The audience was eagerly waiting for Piaf and Pills. The performance would start with me singing three chansons. The tension was immense in the wings and no wonder. We were already twenty minutes late, yet there was no sign of the lovebirds. The spectators were becoming visibly impatient.

'But why aren't they here?' groaned M Lambroso who had organised the evening, and he had every reason to groan. The spectators were stamping, and shouting, 'Begin . . . begin.'

'With what and with whom?' cried M Lambroso, giving me a look that said, all I have is this fellow.

At last Piaf and Pills arrived arm in arm completely sloshed, laughing and swaying on their feet. They tried to explain in thick voices why they were late.

'They served a little white wine at dinner that floated down our throats just like that,' explained Pills.

Holding on to him and hardly able to stand Piaf added, 'We filled ourselves with it.'

Lambroso looked like a shattered man. Even I had never seen Piaf as drunk as that. Moreover, the audience was becoming really furious. I saw only one way out, namely to announce Pills at the end of my song, thus giving Piaf time to sober up a little.

'Are you mad?' burst out Piaf. 'It's me who announces him. He's my man. You, Charles, have nothing to do with it.'

Deeply moved by her words Pills tried to embrace her, but as he moved forward he lost his equilibrium, and it was only the quick intervention of a stage hand that saved him from falling flat on his face.

'I'm going on,' I said to Lambroso. 'You can't keep them waiting any longer. At the end of my three songs I'll announce Pills, and in the meantime try to sober them up, and explain to Piaf that as an exception I will be the one to announce her man.'

I went on stage, and the audience's reaction plainly showed that they were waiting for the next turn, so the quicker I finished the better for all of us. A spectator shouted, 'The next one.'

I was ready to vanish when Lambroso called, 'Stay there, they aren't ready yet.'

'The audience will lynch me,' I called back.

'Never mind. Do it for me.'

I turned to Robert Chauvigny, Piaf's pianist, who luckily knew many of my songs. I gave him three more titles, and I sang the chansons, but it wasn't difficult to see that the audience had had more than their share of me. The noise made my voice almost inaudible, but Lambroso continued to make signs. Pills hadn't recovered completely yet.

What was I to do? I had no more chansons left, so I started telling funny stories which didn't seem funny to the spectators. God be praised, Pills appeared at long last. I announced him, and from the wings Piaf hissed, 'Judas! Rotter! Traitor!'

'They'll set the house on fire', moaned Lambroso.

I sent friends into the auditorium to shout for encores when Pills had finished his last song in order to give Piaf more time to recover. Thus Pills remained on the stage till the interval.

After the interval I announced Piaf who came on the stage, swaying. She lost a shoe on her way to the mike, but managed to pick it up. She sang beautifully. We in the wings looked at each other in utter bewilderment.

'*Marchi les blaches gormenettes, en assis et les gailla nadam,*' she sang.

'But it's gibberish,' groaned Lambroso.

'She's wonderful,' cried Pills in ecstasy.

'If the spectators understand that she means *Marchant pardessus les tempêtes assis sur le gaillard d'avant,*' I observed, 'I'll pay for drinks all round.'

Nevertheless, the audience was as impressed as Pills. They thought she was singing in English. Wasn't she just back from the States? She winked at us, the wink meaning, 'You see how they eat out of my hand?' She was too optimistic.

The second chanson was as incomprehensible as the first. The trouble came with the third. The orchestra started up, Piaf opened her mouth, and not a sound emerged. With short little steps she dragged herself to the piano, leaned against it and said, 'I'm fainting.' The audience exploded, some shouting, 'She's ill!' others, 'She's drunk!' Quickly the curtain was let down. Then I appeared in front of the curtain, saying, 'Ladies and gentlemen, Edith Piaf has had a sudden malaise, the doctor is with her, and he assures us that she'll very shortly be strong enough to continue her repertoire.'

That calmed them down, with one exception. 'You're telling me,' shouted a voice.

At last she reappeared. The audience received her coldly, but once again there came the Piaf miracle. The spectators warmed up, her voice enchanted them, and to make amends she gave them an extra hour of chansons. The final applause was tremendous. When she came off I naturally expected a word or two of thanks since it was I who had twice saved the situation. She went past me without even glancing at me, then fell into Pill's arms, saying, 'Thank you, *chéri*. You saved the situation.'

Years later she came to see me in my dressing room at the Alhambra to invite me to dinner. When I reminded her of that famous evening in Royat, she said with a smile, 'Oh, I did know that you saved the performance, but you know what I'm like when I'm in love.'

The tour took us to the Riviera, where we appeared in Cannes, Antibes, Nice, Monte-Carlo, Fréjus and Sainte-Maxime, but we made our headquarters in a hotel in Cannes so as to be in the centre of it all. Piaf had a whole suite, whereas I had a tiny room on the top floor. Generally she was in a rotten mood on the Riviera. It was a hot summer, and when I looked in on her I usually found her in her nightdress, perspiring profusely. On one such visit she suddenly burst out, 'Swine, selfish bugger, you've been swimming.'

'What's wrong with swimming?'

Because I went swimming and enjoying myself while she worked hard for the lot of us, killing herself for us. Then she became reasonable, and asked me to fetch her a bottle of beer. Through an open door I saw her secretary, Pills and Roland Avelys who was also a member of the troupe, sitting on the floor near the window, letting the sunbeams burn their legs. That was as near as Piaf allowed them to get to the sun. For according to her the sun killed one's vitamins. Whenever we turned night into day in the local nightclubs she dragged us back to the hotel at dawn lest the sun contaminate us.

I sighed my relief when we returned to Paris. As we were going shortly on to America we had to turn night into day in Paris too. One night we were up on the Butte, and while looking for a taxi we saw a giant of a man breaking the chain he had put round his chest by inflating that part of his anatomy. That street performer looked like a real Hercules. A few passersby had stopped to watch him. However, Hercules was almost breathless after he had broken the chain. He was quite old and definitely under-nourished.

'He reminds me of my father,' said Piaf in a broken voice.

I didn't care for that at all, and how right I was. When the poor man approached us with a plate in his hand, he said, 'What an honour for me to have done my miserable act in the presence of a great artiste like you.'

Piaf opened her handbag from which she took twenty thousand francs, which was a lot of money at the time, and put them into the plate. The eyes of Hercules nearly popped out. He just couldn't believe that all that money was meant for him.

'How much have you on you?' she asked as we walked away.

'Not enough to take a taxi.'

We had to walk back the whole way from the Butte to Boulogne, a stroll of seven kilometres, and when we reached the house she said the walk had done her a lot of good, so we would do it every night. Of course it never was repeated.

She had taken to table turning, and when we left for New York she insisted on taking her special table with us. But it couldn't be found among the luggage on our arrival in the New York hotel. She sent me out to buy one. The shops were closing, and I just succeeded in buying a table before the store called Bloomingdales closed its doors. The first thing I saw when I got back to the hotel with the table was the table she thought she had lost.

'You'll look after both the tables,' she said.

Piaf and Pills got married while we were in New York. Marlene Dietrich was present at the wedding. Piaf sincerely admired her, often repeating that it was astounding that a genuine lady like Marlene could become such an intimate friend of hers. It was always a curious sight to see those two so differently built women moving side by side in the street.

'For once I haven't made a mistake,' said Piaf after we had left the register office. I had heard her say that every time she fell in love. We, her close friends, have been accused of behaving like yes men in her presence. The fact was that we didn't contradict her because we didn't want any scenes which always took more out of her than out of those who contradicted her. To say yes was a form of protecting her. In her innermost self she knew perfectly the truth about herself. When she closed her eyes it wasn't only to dream: it was not to see what she didn't want to. Also to forget.

Generally she liked closing her eyes. She lived in a closed world, the curtains were drawn, with as little daylight permitted as possible, and she came to life only at night. I am the contrary in every sense, for I like the sun, fresh air, great spaces and daylight. At our first meeting she had said, 'I like you because you bite into words the same way as I.' But they weren't the same words.

Our similar taste in chansons had brought us really together. Neither for her nor for me was the chanson a means of existence, but a way of living with all its pleasures, dogmas and even moral basis. Nowadays many of the newcomers in the world of the chanson don't manage to hold the floor for long. The reason, I think, is that they are more interested in their bank accounts than in their act, an awful mistake because ours isn't a trade like any other trade. Maurice Chevalier once said to me, 'One enters it as one enters a religion.'

Of course, you can make a great amount of money if you succeed as a chansonnier, but even with a great amount of money life isn't as easy as all that in our profession. For years I lived above my means after my first triumphs, was in debt, was late in paying my taxes, at moments there wasn't a penny in my pockets, yet the papers called me a millionaire. In private life as on the stage an artiste has to put on a big act, a bluff. The successful artiste drives an expensive car, but has to skip a meal to be able to buy petrol.

Yes, one bluffs in every sense. One lies about the fees one is paid, the number of spectators, and especially about one's future plans. Yet when the telephone bell rings one rushes to pick up the receiver in the hope of a contract being offered, and one accepts it even if it is well below the figure one boasts of.

Slowly, I began to understand that my great luck was being my own interpreter. I didn't have to look for new chansons because I could write them myself, or for a singer to sing them as I could sing them myself.

However, my thoughts weren't as clear as that yet on the day Piaf and Pills got married in New York. In fact, I felt I wasn't progressing in my career. True, my name as a writer of chansons was known more and more, but no engagement of big value had come my way to date. Before returning to Paris I took a decision, namely to find myself a home, be it ever so humble, outside Paris where I could work and love undisturbed.

After my return to Paris Raoul Breton and his wife invited me to their country house at Mère. After lunch we strolled in the orchard, and Breton and I talked of our love of the country-side. I said, 'When I'm rich I'm going to leave Paris for good, and buy a house in the country.'

'But you are rich, Charles. Buy one at once. The price of real estate gets stiffer every day.'

'Nobody knows better than you that I haven't a centime. Everybody tells me I'll be rich some day, but at the moment my wallet is still empty. I owe you a pretty large sum.'

Breton replied that my owing him a large sum was proof that he had faith in my future. Having said that he took me in his car to the mayor of the village to find out whether any suitable property was for sale in the neighbourhood. The mayor had nothing to offer. Yet every time I came to stay with the Bretons I roamed the countryside, looking for some house or cottage that might be to my liking.

One day I came on a grange that was practically in ruins. I found it splendid. Behind it were small out-buildings, ruins too, but ruins of solid stone. The remaining walls were thick. Over-excited by my discovery I rushed back to Breton to speak to him about *my* grange. What worried me mostly was that there wasn't a sale notice on any of the buildings. Breton told me not to worry, he would look into the matter and get in touch with the owner.

I went back to Paris in a state of excitement, seeing myself as a landowner who is followed round his acres by his huge dog, prunes his fruit trees, and in winter sits in front of a blazing log fire, entertaining his friends and smoking a pipe.

'It isn't for sale,' said Breton the next day.

I was crestfallen, no huge dog, no pipe. Then I shrugged my shoulders since so many other dreams of mine hadn't come true either.

'If you let me carry on,' said kind Breton, 'I'll speak to a house agent in the district, and instruct him to get in touch with the owner of the ruins and persuade him to sell.'

The dream was on again, and the following Saturday I drove hell for leather to Breton's country house, but as it was much too early to call on him I went to have another look at the grange. The name of the village was Galluis. Daniel Gelin and Danielle Delorme had lived there once. The village boasted two châteaux, one bakery and one café, a quiet, clean village.

I drove to Breton who had just finished his breakfast. He took me to the house agent who was a woman, a very loquacious woman, and she didn't let me put in a word edgeways while she lectured on country properties, and showed me photographs of houses I wasn't interested in.

'I want the grange,' I said, when she let me speak at last.

'But a person in your position can't live in a ruin. And think of all the repairs you'll have to make.'

She continued in that vein, and again she showed me photographs of other houses.

'Anyhow, I haven't a franc,' I said, which frightened her, but Breton reassured her that he would help me.

When she saw she couldn't reason with me she said I was right to stick to my idea, so many clients couldn't make their minds up, in brief she would do all she could to acquire the grange for me.

She got it for a comparatively low sum. Slowly I restored the grange and the outhouse. In fact, it took me four long years before I could call it my home. Several forebears of mine didn't even have a tomb of their own.

I had parted from Piaf on none too good terms when I returned from New York. Although she had sent me a cable saying, 'I miss you,' I decided to put an end to our professional relationship.

'High time,' said Breton. 'You must strike out on your own. I'm fond of Edith, but if you continue moving in her circle it won't get you anywhere in the long run. If you stay in her orbit and remain one of her inner circle it'll do you more harm than good. Professionally you ought to forget her. Look at Gilbert Bécaud. He's beginning to make a name. Why? Because he's free and has no obligations. He's married Kiki, leads a quiet life, and doesn't chase round the world like you. His one aim is to become a star of the chanson in his own country.'

Breton, I thought, was surely right, but on the other hand I had come back from America completely broke, and there was something else too. Piaf was the great pole of attraction, and all those who swarmed round her had gone out of their way to be pleasant and helpful to me because I belonged to her entourage and was her constant companion. I would receive no more friendly smiles now that I was outside her orbit. Since those smiles had been meant more for her than for me, I felt in my bones they would all turn their backs on me. Naturally, they believed that it was Piaf who had got rid of me, tired of me, and it didn't enter their heads that it was I who had taken the decision of leaving her troupe.

While I was with Piaf I made no new contacts in the world that promotes chansonniers. I had friends like Marcel Achard, men of talent, but they were purely companions, and could in no sense further my career. All doors closed on me when it got round that I worked with Piaf no longer, as if to warn me that I was nothing and nobody without her.

With Piaf I sang only in the first half of the show; the second half was totally hers. I could never become a star while I toured with her, but I did manage to scrape a living.

Here is the sort of thing people said about me after my decision to part professionally from Piaf. 'Aznavour is unsaleable. With his figure and voice it is sheer madness to try to conquer the public. It is cheek too. Luckily those who count in the profession know their job, and are determined to keep him out. He won't succeed in any case as he hasn't the necessary talent to do so.'

They weren't any kinder in my presence. 'An Armenian knows how to count, so why don't you become an accountant?'

I fully appreciated that being no more in Piaf's wake was akin to being executed in public. Nobody asked me why I had left her. My need for independence and liberty was proof to them of her having kicked me out. And why did she get rid of me? Because I had no talent. As I was on my own now they could go for me without incurring Piaf's wrath.

'The swine!' said Jean-Louis Marquet indignantly.

'Oh no, I'm not,' I said.

Since my return to Paris not a single offer came my way. Truly all doors were closed, and nobody had time to see me and listen to me even for a minute. Nobody wanted to give me a chance, nobody admitted that I had any talent. If anybody ran into me in the street all I received was an ironic smile and the sort of advice that makes no struggling creative artiste happy.

'What's the good of hanging on, old man? Don't be so obstinate but find something else. Anyhow, ours is an overcrowded profession, full of people without any talent, so why join the rank of the unsuccessful, embittered, jealous and failed chansonniers? Be reasonable.'

They nearly succeeded in convincing me, but my pride wouldn't let them. However, pride doesn't provide you with food and money, and I was deeply in debt. God be praised, I could still go and have my meals with my parents.

And yet, Jean-Louis Marquet was the one person who came to understand me in that terrible period. He knew and appreciated my ambition.

'Piaf predicted a great career for me,' I said to him. 'She isn't the woman to praise if she doesn't mean it. Raoul Breton stands by me, believes in me, and he wouldn't have lent me so much money if he had doubted my talent. Charles Trenet comes often to see me, and encourages me at all our meetings. He isn't a man to waste his time either.'

I thought of Maurice Chevalier too who had never failed to encourage me, who understood I was blazing a trail of my own.

Even so I felt I wasn't getting anywhere, and one must, after all, survive one way or another. Suddenly, I decided to quit. It was a reasonable decision to take. It seemed to me that one can't spend an entire lifetime trying to become a star. If one can't get contracts and the public isn't interested one should call it a day. I had seen enough failures in the profession, and there is nothing as sordid and sad as the singer who reaches the ripe age of fifty still believing that he will become a great star some day. I didn't want to turn into such a pathetic sight. I still meet today some who say, 'I've got a wonderful repertoire of songs. If I find a manager who wants them my success will be enormous.' What those grey haired men forget is that the public must want them too.

My case was different. The impresarios and the public didn't want me because I was no longer with Piaf. And that was worse than sin in their eyes.

I went to see Breton, and said to him that I was calling it a day. Though I would continue writing songs from time to time my public singing was over. I would look for a different occupation.

'What do you want to do?' he asked.

'I'll try being an agent, and discover and look after young talent.'

'If you want to look after young talent look after yours in the first instance.'

'But nothing happens!' I cried. 'Nothing comes my way!'

'It'll come.'

'I don't want to wait till I'm a hundred years old.'

'You won't have to wait that long.'

'Raoul, it's easy for you to speak, but there's no fight left in me.'

'All I ask from you,' said my dear friend, 'is to hold on for another year. If nothing comes your way during that year then do whatever you want to.'

I accepted that. It was like a bet with fate, and in any case it suited my inclinations and dreams. Looking back, I feel certain that in my heart of hearts I never intended to chuck my profession. When I said to Breton that I wanted to it was only a cry of despair.

Every day I went to Breton's office, arriving early in the morning to write chansons and offer them to any singer who was willing to sing them. Many were, and as author I had no cause to complain. In a couple of years—or so it seemed—I would be the owner of a tidy little fortune. Aznavour, the author, was much appreciated: Aznavour, the singer, had to sing for himself only.

Now and again I saw Piaf in secret. Of course, we had made it up, but Breton watched out lest she drew me into her orbit once more.

'The best way for you to get on,' he said, 'is to keep away from Piaf. As long as you're under her thumb you won't have any real friend of your own. If you have a chanson you think she'd like to sing take it to her by all means, but that should be all. You must remain free.'

I had written a chanson with Florence Véran entitled *Je haïs les dimanches* (I hate Sundays) which I thought now would suit Piaf perfectly. So Florence and I—we still shared the apartment in the rue Villaret-de-Joyeuse—went with it to Boulogne to see her.

I hate Sundays
And the ones who change their shirts
And wear nice suits
The ones who get up early
To go fishing
The ones who sleep twenty hours
'Cos there's nothing to stop them
The ones for whom it is the day
To go to the cemetery
And the ones who make love
As they've got nothing else to do
They will envy our happiness
As I envy their happiness
To have Sundays
To believe in Sundays
To like Sundays
When I hate Sundays

'You want me to sing this?' she asked after she had read it.
'Why not?'
'You must be mad.'
'We wrote it for you.'
'For me or not for me you can shove it up your arse.'
'Does that mean that I can do with it whatever I want?'
'Didn't I say so?'
'Quite,' I said, 'but don't come and tell me later that I didn't show it to you.'

I said that because I knew Piaf inside out.

Florence Véran and I withdrew.

Friends had spoken to me about a girl who sang chansons very well, and had a definite style that was completely hers. She sang in a club called la Rose Rouge in Saint-Germain-des-Près. I went to that club after Piaf had refused to sing *Je haïs les dimanches*. The girl kept me waiting till the cabaret closed at a late hour.

'You want to show me a song?' she asked in that voice of hers that charmed everybody.

'Yes.'

'What's the title?'

'*Je haïs les dimanches.*'

She found that a fascinating title, and I sat down at the piano to play and sing it for her. She took it without hesitation. The following day I went to see Raoul Breton to impart the good news. He had the girl put on the list of the *Concours de la Chanson* which was to take place at Deauville. He believed that the girl had a good chance of winning the first prize. Indeed, she won the first prize for interpretation, and her meteoric career began.

The girl was Juliette Greco.

There was something strange and ironical in my meeting her, giving her the song that suited her talent, and persuading her to go to Deauville. Hadn't I said to Breton that I wanted to become an impresario and look after young talent? I would have been, had I persisted, the foremost producer of chansonniers in France. Nowadays there are dozens of

123

producers since we live in an age in which one person has to produce the other. At times producer and produced could easily change places.

On the very day I drew Breton's attention to Juliette Greco Breton had a piece of good news for me.

'I made a date for you,' he said, 'with Tezé, the artistic director of Thompson-Ducretet who is willing to record some of your chansons.'

That was definitely a move in the right direction. Tezé received me charmingly, such a change after my recent experiences! He recorded two chansons of mine, *Jezebel* with Frank Pourcell's orchestra and *Poker*, with Paul Mauriat's orchestra. A small victory, though it brought me no nearer to contracts. The lack of money was becoming catastrophic. Again and again I had to go to Breton, asking him to help me out. It always went like this:

'Raoul, I need money.'

'How much this time?'

'Quite a lot, but you know that in six months time I will be receiving my royalties.'

'Yes, yes, but how much?'

'A hundred thousand francs.'

Breton had a coughing fit. Already I had noticed that the bigger the sum I asked for the longer the coughing fit lasted. If I needed a million he would cough his lungs out.

'Let me discuss it with the Marquise,' the Marquise was his wife, 'and come back on Monday for the answer.'

He never failed me.

When Juliette Greco won her prize I, the composer of the chanson, was told to choose between a medal and seventy-five thousand francs. I chose the seventy-five thousand francs. I needed them more than the glory of a medal.

On my return from Deauville Piaf summoned me. She received me in an angry mood.

'Wretch,' she shouted, 'so now you give my chansons to existentialist singers?'

'But, Edith, you told me I could shove it.'

'I? I never said that.'

'You did.'

'It wasn't the same chanson.'

'It was exactly the same.'

'Then you changed it.'

'I changed nothing. Anyhow, you said you definitely didn't want it.'

'You said, you said . . . you got me wrong, that's all.'

In no circumstances would she have admitted that she had made a mistake when she refused *Je haïs les dimanches*.

'It's a pity,' I said in order to soothe her, 'you refused it because I'd have loved to hear you singing it. But now it's too late.'

'Why is it too late?'

'Because Greco sings it.'

'Greco, Greco. All you can talk about is Greco. Are you in love with her?'

'Not in the slightest. I hardly know her.'

'You are in love with her. Nevertheless, I'm going to sing it, and show your existentialist how it should be sung.'

Frankly, I couldn't complain of the success of the chansons I wrote. Piaf, Greco, Bécaud and many other well known names triumphed with them, but I, the singer remained unemployed. The year Breton had asked from me was nearing its end.

Chapter Ten

Only a few days were left when a small contract dropped miraculously out of the blue, ably helped by Raoul Breton.

There was a music hall called the Pancra in the vicinity of the Bastille, a small music-hall with only three hundred seats. Breton had worked hard to get an engagement for me. Only chansonniers of modest standing sung there, but Breton felt that to be engaged even for a short while would be an opening for his protégé. Anyway, I was better known now because of the songs I had written than the usual run of performers at the Pancra.

The money was no attraction as for three days one got only the meagre sum of nine thousand francs. (When I speak of francs I mean old francs.) The pianist was paid much more, namely fifteen thousand francs. The singers accepted the small fees because the important thing for them was to be seen and heard.

On the first of the three nights I sang at the end of the first part. On the second I was asked to be the star of the evening, but I refused, saying 'I don't want to be the star.' On the third night the same request was made, and I refused again. My reason for refusing was my hope of being discovered at my own value. I wasn't discovered. My misfortune was that at every performance some other singer sang of whom it was said that he was one of the up-and-coming stars. Nobody ever said that of me. Yet I had hoped they would, and that was why I refused to be the star, for the star is past being discovered.

When the three nights were up I found myself exactly where I had started. No agent had come forward to sign me up. Yet plenty of agents came to Pancra on the Friday night, and most of the singers were given a contract for the whole year on the Monday. Mme Pancra liked my chansons very much and my way of singing them, yet it didn't get me anywhere.

Or so I thought when I made my last bow at the Pancra. But a few days later impresarios did get in touch with me, and I began to earn modest sums singing in nightclubs. Admittedly that wasn't much, but at least I could start earning my living again, and on my own, that is not in Piaf's wake.

Speaking of Piaf, she suddenly decided that she wanted me back not only in her life but in her house too.

'Come back,' she said.

If I had listened to my heart alone I would have said yes at once, for it was no good pretending to myself that I had enjoyed my life away from her. But there was Raoul Breton, my real benefactor, and it would have been unfair and unjust to take a decision without his approval. I expected him to disapprove. To my great pleasure and relief he wasn't against it.

'During your lean year,' Breton said, 'you proved to the profession and yourself that you can survive without needing a chaperone. You can, therefore, if you feel like it return to that dangerous world of hers. In my opinion there's no fear of your getting completely under her sway again, and if you find you get fed up you can get out without feeling lost.'

Nothing had changed in Piaf's house. One was always under the impression of being in a station waiting room. People came and went, suitcases lay everwhere, most of them unpacked. She was as tyrannical as of yore, but now I became the exception. When I say that nothing had changed I don't include the lovers, who did change from time to time.

Every night as in the past we found ourselves in the kitchen, where we sat drinking wine or beer for long hours. Nobody was allowed to leave the kitchen except me whom she treated with gentle understanding. If I had my fill I got up from the kitchen table, and went to bed or out, in short I did as I wanted.

'You're going to bed?' she asked on the first night of my return.

'Yes, Edith. I want to work tomorrow morning.'

All present thought she would start shrieking at me.

'You're perfectly right, *génie con*,' which was her usual way of addressing me. 'Go and rest to be in top form when you sit down to work. Good night.'

If I said I was going out because I had a date with a girl she called her chauffeur, and told him to take me in the car. I said I didn't want to keep the chauffeur up, so she said the chauffeur should stay behind, and the car was at my disposal. In vain I protested that I didn't need the car, she remained adamant, and in the end I drove off to collect future memories.

Generally, I drove to the Butte-Montmartre, which nowadays is sadly overrun by tourists in coaches and on foot, and bogus painters try to sell bad imitation Utrillos, but in the early fifties it was still a meeting place of artists and artistes. The cabarets and nightclubs remained as picturesque as they had been before the war. I usually drove up the rue Lepic at breakneck speed, but slowed down reaching the rue Norvins in order to look at the women, and there were plenty of pretty women on the Butte at night.

I was often accompanied on those expeditions by Jean-Louis Marquet and Richard Marsan. We went to Geneviève, then to Attilio, followed Nicole Rey whose singing I enjoyed, and from her cabaret we crossed the street to Pomme. We drank copiously. In the small hours Florence Véran would arrive to control her Richard's fidelity so to speak, and to persuade us it was time to go home. But we had no intention of going home, the night being too young for that. The next stop was the Cloche d'Or which was always crowded at dawn. It was daylight by the time we left it. There followed breakfast in some café, then we went our respective ways completely sobered up.

'Have you found an idea?' Piaf asked when I got back.

'It doesn't come as easily as that, which is one of the reasons why I must go back to the Butte again. You know how it goes. One hears a word, and round that word one weaves a story. Then the chanson is born.'

Now and then Piaf accompanied me to the Butte. That raised my prestige in women's eyes. They erroneously believed I was Piaf's lover, and nothing flatters a woman's vanity more than pinching a famous woman's lover. If I said to a new pickup, 'I'll take you to Piaf's house,' she never refused. My love affairs were sharp and short. I may not be Don Juan, but I wasn't Romeo either. Inside most men there sleeps a Casanova, and my sleep was always very light. Piaf could kill any of my love affairs with one sentence if she felt like it. She often did. She couldn't stand my girl friends if she saw I got on well with them.

'The girl's sweet,' she said, 'but she gets on my nerves.'

She accepted my love affairs only when she was in love herself. Then she said, 'I'm getting married. You two ought to do the same.' When she changed her mind she expected me to change mine too. Anyway, I wasn't thinking of marriage.

I used to love passionately, no love affair of mine was serene or placid, yet they never influenced my chansons, that is to say they never were autobiographical.

No, I wasn't thinking of getting married again, so it was the sheer curiosity of seeing a new face that made me accompany Roland Avelys, who was living in Piaf's house too, to Fouquet's in the Champs-Elysées one afternoon.

'I'm meeting a young woman singer,' he had said, 'with whom I worked in Lyons. She's just come back to Paris. Do come with me, it won't take long. She's very attractive.'

Hence my curiosity, which always gets me into trouble.

Suffice it to say that this girl eventually became my second wife, that we were later divorced, and I have nothing to say about it. Everyone who has had a failed marriage will understand. The only constructive thing she ever did which has lasted, was to introduce me to the young couturier Ted Lapidus, who is still a friend and still makes many of my clothes.

Fortunately, I have been very lucky in my third—and present—marriage, and have three lovely children of it. With my warm Armenian background I have always been a family man. I love children. My first child, my daughter Patricia, has always been close to me. But I had another child too, which is a sad and dramatic story.

While I was still living with Piaf we went one morning to buy herrings. The herring buying expedition ended up that night in a nightclub called La Roulotte. There I met a charming young dancer with whom I remained for four days. On the fifth day I left with Piaf on one of her American tours, and when we returned to Paris I sought the girl out. She told me she was pregnant.

'I'll do all you want me to do,' I said, and paid for the nursing home and all other expenses.

She came to see me after the child was born—it was a boy—and said, 'There's somebody who wants to marry me, but I want you to marry me.'

I said that four nights weren't a basis for marriage.

'In that case you'll never see me again,' she said.

I didn't even know her family name.

Years later I found a letter from her in my letterbox.

'I am getting a divorce,' she wrote. 'I've told your son, Patrick, about you. Drop me a line if you want to see him. If you don't want to that won't be a problem for either of us.'

Of course, I wanted to see my son. She brought the little boy and I took to him—the least a father can do. I said to the mother, 'Now that you're on your own you'll surely want to marry again. If the child is in the way I'm only too willing to take him.'

She agreed, and he came to live with me. He died mysteriously at the age of twenty-five in 1977, that is to say I never found out what he died of. There was a post-mortem, but it revealed nothing. He had gone to bed, and didn't wake up in the morning. He had been a solitary youth, and imagined he had all sorts of diseases. He took pills, and if I wanted to take him to a doctor he refused to go, saying all doctors were crazy. Yet he was intelligent, but I repeat liked to be alone. One day he said he wanted to live all on his own in a little room somewhere. I agreed, and rented a room for him.

He died in that room.

After my three performances at the Pancra small engagements slowly trickled in. 'People must see you,' said Breton. 'They mustn't forget that little face of yours.' I accepted anything that came my way. It didn't bring in any substantial sums, but people began to get accustomed to my little face. Not everybody liked it.

Here is an example. I was engaged to sing in a cinema in Belleville, a far from distinguished or expensive district of Paris. That was in the year 1954, so I was getting on to be thirty. I was to sing six chansons, leaving the one I liked most to the end. All six had already been a success sung by other singers. When I had finished the fifth chanson the audience burst into thunderous applause. However, the applause wasn't in praise of me: it meant I should get off the stage. After the applause they threw things at me, and whistled and hissed. The worst of it was that there wasn't a stage door, one had to leave through the auditorium. I went through the auditorium with my head bent and with fear in my heart. There was no cause for fear: they took no notice whatever of me. They had already forgotten the singer they wanted to get rid of. And I said to myself again that I was an accursed singer, and right were they who declared I wouldn't get anywhere. But then I remembered that Breton, Piaf and

Trenet believed in me. That was a consolation, nevertheless the public's ire or (almost worse) indifference made me despair on such occasions.

Fulfilling those poor man's contracts was hard work indeed. In the course of one night I had to sing in five different places. The spectators' reactions weren't my only worry. When it came to the fifth performance I hadn't any voice left. In the Échelle de Jacob in the rue Jacob in Saint-Germain-des-Prés I had to sing without a mike, and the Echelle de Jacob was the night's last appearance. I overheard somebody saying, 'You see how right I was. The man has no voice at all.'

It was a hard struggle. Now and then I was given a pianist who wouldn't have earned his living even in the days of the silent films. When it was all over I went up to the Butte to find consolation in the company of my friends.

'How did it go?' they asked.

'Definitely better than last night. They even wanted an encore. But with the awful pianist who accompanied me I couldn't take the risk. It would have spoiled my success.'

Did they guess that I was lying? Perhaps they didn't, and in any case a creative artist is entitled to play with the truth.

In those days of struggle I wasn't living with Piaf any more. My second wife, Evelyne and I had moved to the Akropolis Hotel at the corner of the rue de Buci and the boulevard Saint-Germain. The rue de Buci is a noisy street market, and the boulevard Saint-Germain is one of the noisiest thorough-fares in Paris. However, the noise didn't interfere with our loving and quarrelling. We were so broke that we cooked on a ring in our hotel bedroom. Naturally, the hotel people didn't care for that, and they wanted to chuck us out once a week at least. Our room smelt of fish, grilled meat, garlic and onion. I am fond of tasty food.

Our constant friend in our Akropolis days was one Claude Figus, a fervent Piaf fan, whom it was impossible to shake off. He had the gift of the gab, and knew how to flatter. He praised Evelyne's beauty, and treated me with the respect due to the greatest chansonnier of France, but Piaf was his overriding passion. If only he could live with her he wouldn't look at anybody else!

Figus had been in love with Piaf from the age of twelve and he adopted me in order to get nearer to his beloved. Ironically, it was he who introduced Piaf to Sarapo, her last lover, and also to a young accordionist called Francis Lai, who later became the famous composer of the music for *A Man and a Woman*.

Figus took us to the theatre one night and after the play to a café. The next day he called on us, and slowly he became part and parcel of our life at the Akropolis. If not with us he did a lot of café-crawling in Saint-Germain-des-Prés. Actually he lived in Bois Colombes, a suburb, and often missed the last train home. From time to time I helped him out with a little money and cigarettes. To thank me he took us one night to a restaurant in the rue des Canettes, La Polka des Mandibules, a charming place where pipes from the wine vaults were connected with every table to enable the customers to draw their own wine. The result was my leaving the restaurant dead drunk. I repeat it was a charming place, and I took to it, meeting my boon companions there regularly. We always left the restaurant very late.

It was a mercilessly cold winter. It snowed heavily. Leaving the restaurant in the small hours with us Figus informed me that he would walk back to Bois Colombes as he had missed the last train. The night was too cold for that, so I said, 'Don't be an idiot. You'll come and spend the night with us at the Akropolis.'

The night porter hardly glanced at us as he muttered, 'Don't make any noise.' Then he closed his eyes again. Three people sleeping in the same room didn't ruffle a Saint-Germain-des Prés night porter in those days.

'There's only one bed,' Figus observed when we entered the room.

'Quite,' I said.

'Will three of us sleep in it?' he asked.

'Oh no. You take a blanket, roll it round yourself, and sleep on the floor.' The floor was carpeted.

Figus first thought he could curl up in an armchair, but ended up on the floor.

'I've the impression that a dog is sleeping beside the bed,' laughed Evelyne.

'A mongrel,' I laughed.

'Mongrels are more intelligent than pedigree dogs,' called Figus from the floor.

'Bark if anybody approaches the door,' I said, switching off the light.

The winter was a long one, so Figus often slept in our room. He and Evelyne used to chat while I fell asleep. He was nobody's fool, and knew that getting into the wife's good graces would help him a lot with the husband.

In a way I made a mistake when I went to live in Saint-Germain-des-Prés. I am not the kind of person that enjoys that so-called existentialist milieu. But that wasn't all. The cabaret and night clubs were small in that district. Take the Echelle de Jacob, with only forty seats, too little space for my dimension. The people who said I wouldn't succeed were people who heard and saw me in those small cabarets. I am made for large stages, that is for plenty of room as I must move about while I sing. I need as much space as a dancer. I can't stay put when I face an audience. I feel like a drowning man if I haven't enough room. I repeat it was a mistake to sing in Saint-Germain-des-Prés. However, the mistake brought in enough money to keep my wife and myself alive.

After a time we stopped going to La Polka des Mandibules which we had found such a charming place in the beginning. When we started drinking there the restaurant was poorly frequented, but slowly it began to fill up, in short became fashionable, and the prices rocketed. From twenty francs the wine rose to a hundred and twenty, the excuse being that well known artistes sang on the premises. Evelyne and I were the well known artistes. Not only were we not paid but had to cough up five times as much for our wine. I forget: we got our cigarettes free.

The Butte-Montmarte remained my real spiritual home in Paris. While Evelyne and I lived in Saint-Germain-des-Prés we often finished our nights up there. Our ports of call remained chez Nicole Ray and chez Geneviève, but Geneviève got an engagement in America, so only Nicole Ray and Pomme on the other side of the street were left. Also we went to Attilio in the rue Norvins.

I was devoted to Pomme, a remarkably intelligent woman with whom one could talk for hours. The striking difference between the Butte and Saint-Germain-des-Prés was the genuinely Bohemian side of the Butte. You could take fellow artistes to any café, sit down at the piano, and play and sing, trying out your chansons on your friends. An immense amount of talent gathered on the Butte, Jacques Brel among them.

Jacques Brel wrote chansons which were still unsuccessful, and he had nowhere to sleep. I suggested he saw an impresario I knew who was sure to take him in for a few nights. Brel was a fundamentally timid person—we used to call him L'abbé Brel—so I had to use all my gift of persuasion to get him to the impresario who told him he would be pleased to put him up. The impresario was a well known homosexual. Brel went to bed late, but the impresario went to bed even later. When Brel heard him arrive early in the morning, he used to jump out of bed, and dress hurriedly, he was so afraid of the impresario making a pass at him.

We were totally different temperaments. Brel said to me, 'When you're angry at someone, you yell and swear. Me—I never do that. I kill them with quiet words.'

Most of my artiste friends on the Butte, beginners like myself, became famous in time. It isn't the same any more on the Butte. The new generation is in too much of a hurry to earn money. Our generation grew up during the Occupation, our life was a life of restrictions. The present generation was brought up on cakes.

Jacques Brel admired Charles Trenet, and so did I. He was one of the masters. If, now, I feel I am the father of plenty of songs and singers, I have a father, too and it is Trenet. Brel's first chansons were influenced by Trenet. We used to talk for hours about the chanson and our respective approach to it. Brel was determined to go his way, although he didn't know yet where it would lead him. Owing to my trips to America I was interested in American songs. I wanted to write personal, autobiographical songs, which would be stories. Perhaps the first song like this was *Brother, Can You Spare a Dime?*—but we hadn't heard it. I knew even then that my originality was in the lyrics, not in the music. My songs are dialogues. Take away the music and you can recite them on stage. When I'm tired, I talk to the music. Once in Lausanne I was totally without voice and I did a concert like that. Recently, they gave me the tape and it is something special. In those days I was still inventing myself.

Brel had his own vision of things. He was a boon companion, and drank as heavily as I. His family was very wealthy, so his approach to his career was strikingly different from mine.

We weren't like present day artistes, for with us public appearances meant more than money. We were cheated by the agents who guessed that we preferred glory to pelf. Nowadays, pelf comes first. One wants to earn money even before one becomes known by the public. With us, it was the other way round.

Chapter Eleven

The tide was turning. It turned, in fact, in the year 1954. I had been an *artiste maudit* till the age of thirty. One can easily say it isn't too bad to have to wait till the age of thirty, but for the one who waits it is a hell of a time. Yet I didn't despair during the waiting period. I felt sure that slowly people would come to understand my approach to the chanson. Fundamentally I was a visionary who firmly believed that the chanson had to change, become more involved, stop ignoring the different social classes, be more personalised, and more personal too. I had felt that in my bones from the moment I embarked on my career. The world would think the same in time, I used to say to myself. And so it happened.

In the old days the chanson was more romantic, and had little to do with reality. I chose reality, that is real situations, and the world followed me. I was the first to write the modern, realistic chansons. Anyhow, the general public isn't interested in who was the first, but before the Italians started writing them, and before the English and the Americans started writing them—the Germans haven't begun yet—mine was the voice crying in the wilderness. They all heard it even though they didn't acknowledge it when they followed in my wake.

I chose subjects that were near the knuckle. It hadn't occurred to anybody before to tell a woman (in the chanson, of course) that she is getting fat or becoming ugly, that she ought to wear more make-up to hide her wrinkles, or that I don't feel like making love to her again.

YOU LET YOURSELF GO

Ah! you are nice to look at
Your tights falling around your shoes
In your old unbuttoned dressing gown
And your curlers, what a state
I ask myself each day
How did you manage to seduce me?
And how did I fall in love with you?
And how could I tie you up forever in my life?
Like that, you look just like your mother
Who has nothing to inspire love

I put every possible human situation into my chansons. If anybody comes to me and says, 'Did you hear that American song about a woman with a big belly because she is going to have a baby?' I can answer that I wrote about that subject twenty-five years ago. I can say without boasting since truth isn't boasting, that I have handled every situation that can arise between men and women. I even went as far as writing about a man loving a man.

AS THEY SAY

As a new day is dawning
I get home to find my bundle of loneliness
I take off my eyelashes and my wig
Like a poor clown, unhappy and tired
I go to bed but I can't sleep

I think of my joyless love
And of that boy, handsome like a God
Who put fire in my mind without even trying
My mouth will never dare
Confess my sweet secret
My tender tragedy
'Cos he is the reason for all my torment
Spent all his time in women's beds
Nobody has the right to judge me or blame me
But I want you to know
That only nature is responsible
If I'm a man, oh! As they say

As I look back on my career I find that the turning point came when due to Breton's secretary I got an engagement in Lisbon for a fortnight. It is food for thought that his first real success came in a foreign country to the singer who had fought and struggled in vain to achieve it in his native land.

The cabaret, where I was to sing, was called the Tajide. I sang the same chansons I had sung many times in Paris, where little notice was taken of them if I sung them myself. In Lisbon the applause was overwhelming, and already on the first night the management asked me to come back the next year.

From Lisbon I continued my journey by car to Casablanca. I arrived in Casablanca with Richard and Florence Véran. Our performance was an hour and a half long. It began with Richard who told a few stories before announcing Florence. She sang several chansons, then sat down at the piano and Richard announced me. I sang accompanied by her. When I had finished I announced Richard and took Florence's place at the piano to accompany his imitations.

On the first night I knew I had achieved the success I had always dreamed of. The next day the newspapers praised me to the sky. The result was a three months contract for the three of us in Morocco, Algeria and Tunis. Though I missed Evelyne badly I fulfilled the engagement, and how right I was! Jean Bauchet, the director of the Moulin Rouge in

Paris, saw and heard me in the Casino of Marrakesh, and offered me a contract at the Moulin Rouge, something I wouldn't have imagined a few months before.

Bauchet said to me, 'I like what you're doing. Couldn't you sing some time at the Moulin Rouge?'

'In what capacity?'

'As the star of the performance.'

I returned to Paris with a sort of halo. Everybody had heard rumours that the accursed singer had triumphed in North Africa, 'So there must be more to him than we thought,' said the same folk who had ignored or laughed at me in the past. Impresarios, who had kept their distance from me, now came running with contracts, enough contracts for a whole year. Nothing like that had happened to me before. Some of them, who had been specially aloof in the old days, I kept waiting which gave me quite a kick. After all, I am human too.

Here I can't resist relating an anecdote. The director of a Brussels cabaret, who had steadily refused to have anything to do with me in the past, came to offer me a contract in his club. I asked for eight thousand francs, he said it was too much. He had been thinking of four thousand francs. The following year he offered eight thousand, but I wanted sixteen thousand as my price was rising with my increasing fame. Too much, was his answer.

'I offer you sixteen thousand,' he said the next year.

'Not enough. I want to be paid more than you pay Piaf.'

Piaf was the highest paid star in the world.

'That's impossible,' he said.

He paid Piaf thirty thousand francs.

'All right,' he said the following year. 'How much more do you want above Piaf's fee?'

'One franc,' I said.

After that I was able to tell my friends that I was better paid than Piaf.

When I got back to Paris after my North African tour I went to Ted Lapidus to order a suit, and bought a large American car on credit.

At the Moulin Rouge my success was overwhelming, that is to say it even overwhelmed me. 'Aznavour has changed,' said friends and enemies to Raoul Breton after the applause at the Moulin Rouge.

'It isn't Aznavour who's changed,' said Breton. 'It is you who have changed.'

Bruno Coquatrix, the high-priest of the music-hall, came to see me. To sing at his music-hall, the Olympia, was the consecration of any chansonnier's career. The Olympia is the only music-hall dedicated to the chanson the whole year round. It is known and respected all over the world. All famous American singers crave for an engagement at the Olympia because singing at the Olympia is the best possible publicity in our profession. The Beatles were at the Olympia when they came to Paris, and Liza Minnelli was discovered on the night she made her début at the Olympia.

'Your repertoire of songs is good,' said Coquatrix on the day he called on me, 'but for your success at the Olympia you need a new chanson, a chanson nobody has heard before.'

After he left I sat down at the piano in my little room in my new apartment in the rue Rustique up on the Butte-Montmartre. Evelyne was out. There was nobody to distract or interrupt me. I was nervous as I don't like to work on command. I smoked a whole packet of cigarettes, yet not an idea came. What, I wondered, could I write about myself or my life? Yes, my life, *sur ma vie*. Within three hours the song was born, its title *Sur ma vie*, which translates into English as *Upon My Life*.

The great evening approached, and my nerves were on edge. Jean-Louis Marquet brought the news that I was being offered thirty-thousand francs a day for a summer tour in the South of France. The offer came from Jean Renzully in Marseilles. But even this didn't calm me.

On the famous evening Renzully was in the auditorium at the Olympia. He hadn't seen me before, and his offer was based on my growing reputation. I came on stage, and started singing. For the first time in his life Renzully heard my veiled voice. He has laryngitis, he said to himself. I continued singing, and the poor man was nearly out of his wits. There was no getting away from it that he had signed on a sick man, and when they heard me sing the good folk of Marseilles would lynch him for having brought a sick man into their town. And what would his wife say?

In his despair he didn't notice how well I was received by the spectators. All he noticed was that my voice was even more veiled in my second chanson. The poor man was convinced that I would die on the stage before the end of the performance. How could he recuperate his money before it was too late? No, that money was lost.

At the end of my fifth chanson I received frantic applause. If they like it here perhaps they will like it on the Canebière too, was the only consolation he could think of. So he applauded as vigorously as the rest of the audience.

For the first time in my life there was a queue outside my dressing room during the interval. Renzully joined the queue, and heard all the high praise that was lavished on me. Of course, I was pleased although I couldn't help remembering the nasty things those same mouths had voiced in the recent past. I did shake hands with many of my erstwhile detractors. Coquatrix had rightly said, 'A singer must be a diplomat too.' Such a lot of people thronged the dressing room that my poor parents were practically pushed into a corner. They at least were sincerely pleased. I had to force my way through dinner jackets and long evening dresses to embrace them before they went home proud of their son.

After my success my father's acquaintances began to address him as Monsieur Aznavour. 'I am Aznavourian,' my father replied. 'It's my son who's Aznavour.'

My wife Evelyne was in the dressing room too, moving from one group to the other drinking in the praise. I regretted that neither my sister who was still in Canada nor Piaf who was singing in New York could be present at the Olympia. However, the Bretons were there, both of them radiant. Hadn't they been the first to believe in me?

At long last the dressing room emptied. I was left with Evelyne, Jean-Louis, Figus and Jean Leccia.

'Where are we going?' they asked.

'To the Cloche d'Or as Piaf always goes there after a first night,' I said.

News travels fast. I was received at the Cloche d'Or like a conquering hero. My dream had come true in every sense. Yet when Evelyne and I went home I was too excited to fall asleep. I got out of bed and wrote a letter to my sister, telling her of my triumph. Then I lay down again, and fell asleep on my freshly cut laurels.

Why, I asked myself after my outstanding success at the Olympia, had public opinion so suddenly changed about me? Perhaps the answer was that the public had got accustomed to me, or maybe my despair at my lack of success had captivated them in the end. But something did happen, and I am the last to understand it or be able to explain it. It is even possible that all of a sudden the public and the critics had sensed my passionate devotion to my profession. My love of the chanson towered above other loves. I chased women, always looking for the ideal companion, though in retrospect it seems that something invariably kept me back from surrendering totally to the love of the moment, probably my love of my profession holding me back from that total surrender. I longed for a peaceful life, but when life was peaceful my art languished, so I had to burst out to find the inspiration I needed.

I loved women till the itch of creating seized me. Then they were in the way. No woman had succeeded in being my muse, though several thought they were.

'You ought to go out,' I would say when I felt like writing a chanson.

'But why?'

'Because I need to be alone to be able to work.'

When the chanson was written I wished she were back. In fact, I was impatient to see her.

'Where have you been? You kept me waiting,' I said.

'But it was you who told me to go out.'

Still, that doesn't explain my popularity that had come like a miracle.

Before it I was afraid I wouldn't succeed; now after my success I trembled lest I didn't live up to it. There are no quiet moments in my profession. With my suddenly found success I nearly envied my unsuccessful past. I though of the bad old days when Patachou, who wasn't yet Patachou only Breton's secretary, shouted 'Don't go into that room. M Trenet is using the piano.' Now it would be, 'M Aznavour is using it.' I had to live up to M Aznavour, which was not as easy as all that. The stage for the chansonnier is like the corrida for the torero. Death comes to the chansonnier in a different form, yet it is death all the same.

I wasn't too indulgent with the journalists who had attacked me and my chansons in the past. Some of them didn't even bother to go to the theatre to hear me, and I am not sure that they took the trouble to hear my records. Nevertheless, they wrote denigrating articles about me, declaring themselves willing to bury me.

My parents were inordinately proud of my triumph. Now and then mother said to father, 'Let's go for a walk.' That meant going as far as the Moulin Rouge or the Olympia to look as the bills with my name blazed across. Of course, I saw my daughter Patricia as often as my travels permitted. I taught her to play the piano, and she had a record player and a vast collection of records. I had to sign a lot of photographs whenever I came to my parents' house, one for the butcher, one for the baker, one for the grocer, for the son of a friend, and for the landlord, such a nice man even if one is late in paying the rent.

Despite my triumph at the Olympia I still didn't manage to control myself when my anger was aroused. Now that I had more elbow-room I accepted Ted Lapidus' suggestion to accompany him to the winter sports in the Alps of Huez. Frankly, I had no idea what winter sports meant or stood for. I arrived at lunchtime, and our table was at the far end of the hotel dining room. Thus I had to cross the entire dining room to reach the table. The other hotel guests were arrayed in sumptuous pullovers, whereas I wore just an ordinary pullover and even more ordinary trousers, in short my driving outfit. I wasn't at my ease, and walking the length of the long dining room was sheer misery.

'I'll leave tomorrow,' I said to Lapidus.

As I was becoming well known many pairs of eyes turned in my direction to stare at me unabashed. That made me more ill at ease, if possible. Nonetheless, I stayed on to please my friend.

One day he brought a gentleman to my room who had travelled five hundred kilometres to see him. The gentleman declared that Mendelssohn was a greater composer than Bach. Everybody is entitled to his opinion, but I admire Bach so much that I took it for a personal insult. I shouted, 'Monsieur, get out of my room if you don't like Bach!'

As the poor man stepped back he knocked against the glass door, and collapsed on the floor. When he rose he rushed from the room. By then my anger had waned, and I chased after him to apologise to tell him he was as much entitled to love Mendelssohn as I to adore Bach. He was already too far away, so I couldn't catch up with him. I swore never to lose my temper again with a person whose tastes were different from mine however ridiculous those tastes were.

But I still get angry when I am professionally illtreated so to speak. For instance if a projector gives the wrong light when I am on the stage, and the management tells me that nothing can be done about it, I decide not to return to that place, and I keep to it.

If the lighting doesn't please me or the curtain isn't to my taste I prefer to sing to a smaller public somewhere else, where I feel I can do my work properly. You aren't entitled to make people enjoy themselves when you don't enjoy yourself. I find that dishonest on the part of the performer. I find too that the performer must sincerely care for his public. The contrary is obtaining something under false pretences. If the performer says to himself that he has forty-five minutes to give the public, not a second more because he has a date with someone at the end of the forty-five minutes he won't be in communion with the public. That is obtaining something under false pretences also. I don't say that I am on the top of my form every time I appear before an audience, but I inevitably reach my form at the third or fourth chanson.

Mine is a lonely profession, for one is always alone when one writes and when one sings. Piaf was lonely and alone; so was Maurice Chevalier, and so am I. How right Chevalier was when he said our profession was like a religion. It is a religion because one has to be in communion with one's public. If one isn't a believer one will never make a career in the world of the chanson. One night my voice was especially hoarse, and after the performance a woman spectator came to my dressing room to say, 'You were excellent tonight. What a pity that your voice was hoarse.' Despite my hoarse voice the woman had felt I was giving my best.

Bruno Coquatrix was always full of new ideas. An international performance at the Olympia was one of them. Sydney Bechet was the American star, Marcel Marceau the French star, and I the Armenian star. He had engaged a Brazilian ballet too to make it even more international. I said to Coquatrix, 'I'd like to sing at the end of the first part. That would suit me and my voice perfectly.'

'You can't,' said Coquatrix. 'The Brazilian ballet will come after you, and it's an extraordinarily good troupe.'

We opened in Versailles, and the Brazilian ballet was a total flop. Coquatrix said immediately afterwards that I could sing at the end of the first part if I wanted.

'I don't want it any more,' I said. 'I'll stay where I am.'

We moved on to the Olympia, and I received wonderful notices probably because the Brazilians bored the press stiff.

When I had ended my three weeks triumph at the Olympia I had to fulfil my engagement with Renzully, who was now completely in love with my sick voice. He rubbed his hands, saying in a strong Marseillais accent, '*Putaing!* I do know how to choose.'

Cannes was the first stop on my tour in the Midi. Now that I could afford it and my new situation demanded it I moved into a luxurious five-star hotel on the Croisette. My worries began as I entered the swing-door of the hotel. How should I tip the page who accompanied me to my large sunny room? Too little wouldn't do, and overtipping would make me look ridiculous in his eyes. Having no idea how much was too little and how much was too much I put my hand into my trouser pocket, and gave him the money I found in it. He bowed too low, and there was a condescending glance in his eyes. I sighed because I saw I still had a lot to learn.

Left alone I went to the window. The view of the sea was magnificent, but it was definitely included in the price of the room. Perhaps, I thought, I ought to have taken a room that gave on an inner courtyard as it used to be when I toured with Piaf. I looked into the bathroom which was twice as large as the room Evelyne and I shared in Paris. I lifted the receiver, and asked for my luggage to be sent up. Then I sat down in an armchair and lit a cigarette. The luggage arrived, I tipped the man, and received a baleful look. I sighed again.

I lit another cigarette, and when I had stubbed it out I became angry with myself, for I had to admit that all that comfort and luxury bored me. What was I to do? To go out and do some shopping wasn't a good solution because I knew myself well enough to be pretty certain that I would buy more than I could afford. I could go swimming, but to swim alone, that is without some goodlooking girl, was no pleasure for me. I went and sat down at the table, spread out paper, took my dictionary of rhymes from a suitcase, and worked. I quickly lost my boredom. Inspiration kept me company and I forgot to eat that night.

The tour continued, and I grew aware that I had become a star that was to stay on the firmament of the chanson. People turned round to look at me in the street, women stopped me to ask for my autograph. A further proof of my new position was the restaurant bills. I had to pay more than ordinary mortals for the same food and wine. In the shops I was treated in a similar manner. I received letters from strangers, asking for loans. I was assured that such letters proved without the slightest doubt that I had gone up in the world.

'When they start touching you for loans and robbing you,' Piaf used to say, 'you know you're on the right road.'

I was definitely on the right road because they came by the dozen to flatter me, to praise me in order to sit at my table and to ask for loans when they had eaten and drunk well. Needless to say, they kept the late-comers out. They weren't people who like sharing. They read my letters before I saw them, and kept me in ignorance if a real old friend wrote to or called on me. I had no opinions left because they voiced theirs as mine. All that was left for me to do was to treat them like an oriental despot his slaves, and they enjoyed that on account of the many advantages they received as slaves. That lasted for a few months.

During the tour I sang one night at the Villa d'Este. When I came off the stage we all went into the kitchen to drink bottles of red wine as in the good old days with Piaf. I picked up a paper, and saw there an article about me. It insinuated that I had become a puffed up, conceited person. That article was like a cold shower. I said I was going back to my hotel alone.

My fourteen hangers on asked in one voice, 'What's wrong, Charles? Aren't you well? Has somebody done something you don't like? Don't forget we're your friends. You know we'll always stand by you.'

I turned back from the door, and said, 'It's nothing. I'm a little tired. Amuse yourselves. Good night.'

I took a taxi, and when I was in my room I stared at my reflection in the mirror.

'You poor fool,' I said to my reflection.

Chapter Twelve

I didn't have to worry about contracts any more. I got all the engagements I could reasonably cope with.

In Vichy I took part in the shooting of a film, my part a small one, singing one of my chansons. From Vichy I drove hell for leather to Menton on the Riviera, where a gala performance was waiting for me.

The year was 1957, and I had been on tour most of the summer with Renzully, the man from Marseilles. That tour had lasted for sixty-five days. I always drove myself, and while on tour I drove many hours at a time. Today one is in Deauville, tomorrow in Monte-Carlo, the day after up in Mégève. Driving such distances is tiring indeed.

I was on my way from Menton to Mégève. I was tired because I had done too much driving during the last two days. A heavy twelve ton lorry loaded with bauxite crashed into my car, and that accident could easily have put an end to my career and myself. When I caught sight of the lorry it was already too late. I tried as hard as I could to hold on to the steering wheel, but my forehead and nose hit the windscreen. I felt a heavy weight on my knees and my legs hurt like hell. Stupidly I prayed that my nose shouldn't be broken as if only my nose was in danger!

I tried to raise my right arm to my face, but it refused to move. So I tried to raise my left arm, but the left arm didn't move either. I looked down to find some explanation for all the pain I felt: my wrist watch hung on the twisted steering wheel. Continuing my investigations I discovered a bone protruding where my elbow had been. It was bleeding. I was still calm in a sense, examining myself and my surroundings as if I were doing it for somebody else. The dashboard had dropped on my thighs which explained the weight I felt on them. I vaguely heard a voice say outside, 'They're all dead.' Suddenly afraid that I might faint before I knew for sure that we were all dead I called Figus and Leccia, my travel companions.

'How are you two?' I asked.

'My hand hurts,' said Leccia who answered first.

'And you Figus?'

'My head is like a stew,' said Figus.

Despite my awful pain I couldn't help thinking that Figus was exaggerating again.

Several people were arriving to rescue us. They managed to get my two companions out of the car, but I remained pinned down by the dashboard. When the rescuers touched me I cried out with pain. So I have broken my arms, I thought. What about the legs? In the meantime I must take the rescue operation in hand.

'Get on the bonnet,' I said to the nearest person, 'then pull the dashboard towards you, but be careful not to cut your hands with the broken glass. I must get out of here as quickly as possible.'

He jumped on the bonnet, and as he pulled the dashboard towards him my eyes were caught by the many coloured electric wires attached to the dashboard. He pulled as hard as he could, but he didn't succeed in dislodging it more than a few inches. So it fell back on my legs. I shrieked with pain, and that pain enveloped my whole body. A second man of good will climbed on the bonnet. By then I was sweating profusely, and I could hardly breathe. The two rescuers pulled at the dashboard, and because there were two of them and had, therefore, managed to pull it farther it hit me with even more strength when it fell back. The pain was such that I couldn't shriek any more.

Figus chose that moment to lean over me and ask, 'Are you all right, Charles?'

Miserable little cunt, I thought, can't you see the lamentable state I am in? As I was going to say some nasty words to him—that is if I had enough strength left—I saw that the two men of goodwill were getting ready to have another go at the dashboard, which was the last thing I wanted after the atrocious pain they had unwillingly caused me.

'Let me do it alone,' I called to them in a faint voice.

Thank God they heard the faint voice, so they left me to my own devices. Slowly, moving inch by inch, taking all the precaution in the world, I managed to crawl out of the car. Then I collapsed on my knees.

I can still hear Leccia complaining bitterly because he had twisted a finger. He moaned that he would never be able to play the piano again. Figus lay on the roadside surrounded by a small crowd, gasping like one who is on the verge of death. Medical examination would show that he had only scratched his nose a little.

I lay down in the grass. My ears were still throbbing with the screeching of the brakes and the noise of the collision. My arms were useless, just deadweight, and I asked myself when the real, terrible pain would begin. I didn't dare to move, but my eyes flitted from one person to the other.

Somebody bent over me, and said, 'Don't worry, old man, the police have been notified, and the ambulance will arrive any minute now.'

But the ambulance was taking its time. In fact it didn't show up. 'We can't let him die like this,' said an onlooker. Another said he would take me in his car to the nearest hospital. It wasn't easy to get me into his car with my hanging arms, and I shrieked with pain as I sat down in it. My kind driver drove fast, afraid that I might die on him, and he repeatedly observed, 'This isn't the right direction.'

Suddenly I caught sight of an ambulance parked on the roadside. Simultaneously the fearful pain I had been waiting for seized me with all its strength. I can't recollect how they got me into that ambulance. My sole memory of the transfer of my aching body from car to ambulance is the nurse tying my arms with bandages to stop them from hanging.

The ambulance took me to the hospital in Brignoles, a journey of fifty kilometres. The press was waiting for me, and in the fog of suffering I vaguely saw the newspaper and cameramen. I don't know how I managed it but I did give them a smile. *Métier oblige.* The show must go on. In the hall of the hospital the pain became so terrible that a nurse had to give me a morphine injection. Before I passed out I asked the -nurse to let my family know about my accident and where I was. My parents and Patricia were in Cannes, my wife in Saint-Tropez.

When I came round I was in plaster from chin to waist. The long waiting began.

I have been asked several times by interviewers when I realised that the public cared for me. My answer inevitably is that I realised it while I lay in plaster in the hospital of Brignoles. For I had received three postal bags filled with letters from my fans the day after the newspapers reported my car accident.

Those letters were a warming and comforting surprise. Frankly, I hadn't imagined that I could mean so much to the people who had heard me singing in the flesh or had listened to my records. Till the accident I had looked on myself as one who had at long last come modestly into his own like so many others. I just didn't look at myself as an annointed star of the chanson. The point is that I had never been the hope of the chanson. Some singers are born hopes. It is said of them already at the start that they will go a long way. As I have said umpteen times in this book only very few had put their faith in me. But the three postal bags full of letters were beautiful proof of the public having taken to me. I am not unduly modest, nonetheless the public's affection was a genuine surprise. I hadn't thought for a moment that my name could mean so much to them, and the letters truly showed there was a special relationship between the public and me.

However, I did receive some anonymous letters, four in all, full of silly nonsense, such as, 'You had a broken voice, now your arms are broken too,' but the others helped me during my long convalescence to endure it with patience.

The public's reaction to my accident was like a spark that starts a fire. They probably said to themselves that Aznavour told their own stories in his chansons. He was one of them, and now they had nearly lost him. They didn't write their letters because I had become a star: they wrote because they were frightened they wouldn't hear me again.

I repeat those letters made me perceive that I hadn't struggled and persevered in vain.

But on the other hand the accident was a disaster for me. It made me lose much time and money. I remained for eighteen months in plaster during which time it was impossible to earn my living. I had my daughter and my wife to keep and I had bought a house. It took me twelve years to pay my debts.

'You won't be able to touch the paino again,' said the first doctor to examine me. Probably he had no idea how miserable his words made me. I made him wait three months for his fee.

'It will all depend on your own efforts,' said the next doctor whom I consulted.

It was a hard fight to get my arms and fingers moving again. One day it seemed I was winning the battle, the next that I was losing it. I can't remember the physical suffering perhaps because I know how to bear pain, but the continuous itching of the arms in plaster nearly drove me mad. I didn't let the nurses help me when I ate. I preferred to stand upright, and leaning against the wall of my room I forced the fork, that is the hand that held it, to my mouth.

My arms were in slings when I sat down at the piano for the first time. I forced my fingers to touch the keyboard. Play or break, I told them furiously.

It took me three years to be able to tie a necktie. I later had to undergo three operations before I could use arms and hands properly. I still have rheumatic pains in my arms from time to time—but so has half of mankind. If somebody comes to me and says how lucky I was I feel like showing him to the door.

Before the accident I had signed a new contract to sing at the Olympia. It had to be postponed, another loss of income.

Faithful Figus remained beside me while I was in hospital. He knew how to earn my gratitude. 'Are you thirsty, Charles?' If I said I was he chased down to the kitchen to get me some mineral water.

'Charles, here's your water.'

'Thank you.'

In the beginning the nurses had offered to fetch the things I needed, but Figus objected, and insisted on fetching and carrying for me. Bringing the water didn't seem sufficient to earn my gratitude.

'The water is too cold I think,' he would say.

'Never mind, hand it over.'

'Don't you think it'll be bad for your vocal cords?'

'Don't annoy me,' I said.

'Don't drink so fast, it's bad for one.'

'Go to hell.'

He sat down disgruntled, thus leaving me in peace for a few minutes, but only for a few minutes. The next move was to pull my sheets, arrange my pillow, see no draught entered through the door or the window, then to fetch a brush to brush my hair.

'Sit down for God's sake or get out of the room,' I burst out.

Deeply hurt he left the room only to return a quarter of an

hour later, and just in time because my skin was itching under the plaster. He took a knitting needle, which he inserted between plaster and skin, and skilfully scratched my skin.

'Like this, Charles?'

'Excellent, go on.'

Shortly before my liberation he brought a friend of his along, Dany Brunet, a tall young man, all muscles, blue eyes and an aquiline nose. He was the battling sort, and immediately I liked him. Figus suggested I take him on as my chauffeur while I wasn't able to drive myself. I took him on, and we set out for Paris, Dany driving, I sitting beside him, Figus in the back with the luggage.

My fingers still didn't respond as I wanted and needed them to respond. The doctors had warned me that they wouldn't be as supple as before the accident. Most depressing, yet I persevered.

Dany proved an excellent find. He was always at my side without anything servile about him. He accompanied me to the Bretons where I saw many old friends again. I wasn't much of a sight with my shaved head and arms still in plaster.

At last the great day came. The plaster was taken off, and I stared at my emaciated limp arms.

'My poor Charles,' exclaimed Figus with tears in his eyes.

'A bit of exercise will do them a lot of good,' said Dany who wasn't easily moved.

I agreed with him, and I summoned Jean-Louis Marquet into my presence.

'You can accept contracts again,' I said.

'Are you able to fulfil them?'

'I must, and that's the most important thing.'

'I've an offer for Algiers, and I'm going to see Coquatrix to arrange your appearance at the Olympia. In my opinion you'll have a full house.'

'Do you think so?'

'I'm certain,' said Jean-Louis. 'Your accident has shown how popular you are. The newspapers haven't stopped talking of you.'

I went back to work.

Figus was called up for military service. A soldier's life didn't suit his artistic temperament, and when I saw him in uniform I couldn't help thinking that the frontiers of France must be pretty vulnerable if all French soldiers were like him. He was stationed in Metz. He telephoned me one morning, full of complaints, the army wasn't for him at all, and he wanted to come to Paris for the weekend, but for that he needed a pass.

'I can't help you,' I said.

'Oh yes, you can. Send me a telegram, saying "I am very ill, I need you. Mother."'

I told him I would send him the telegram. I asked Dany to take it to the post office.

'It begins with telegrams,' said Dany, 'then come postal orders, caviare and foie gras.'

That telegram was followed by other telegrams during Figus' military service. All his relations took it in turn. Grandmother was on her death bed, a brother had an accident, a cousin broke a leg, and an old uncle was waiting for him, to give up the ghost.

Army life hadn't cured him of his servility. 'Your hair's dirty,' he said to me when he reappeared in Paris. 'Nobody looks after you. Nobody thinks of sending you to the hairdresser.'

He still saw himself as the great singer of tomorrow. He used to climb over the barracks wall at night to sing in a small cabaret near the station. That, he said, was how he earned his living, his soldier's pay being not enough even for cigarettes.

'Then why do you ask me for money every time you come to Paris?' I asked.

'Because I can't earn my living every night.'

'Why not?'

'Because on most nights,' he said with dignity, 'I'm under arrest.'

When he had finished his military service I made him the happiest man on earth. I introduced him to Piaf.

'Stop that balls,' said Piaf when he started paying her fulsome compliments.

A few weeks later he appeared in my room like one who has seen a ghost or maybe Death itself.

'What's happened now?' I asked.

'I proposed to Piaf, and she had a laughing fit.'

He was dangerously in love with Piaf. When I say dangerously I mean dangerously for himself. He wanted to do something spectacular to draw her attention to him. He bought a frying pan and an egg which he took to the Arc de Triomphe, and when he was under the arc, he broke the egg in the pan, and held it over the flame above the tomb of the Unknown Soldier. The egg just started sizzling as a police-man appeared, grabbed the sacrilegious Figus, and took him to the nearest police station. He managed to get in touch with me from the police station to ask me what he should do. I called my lawyer who told me it might cost Figus a stiff prison sentence. He was let out next morning, and when he appeared in the magistrates' court he was given three months. Figus decided to appeal against the sentence. I tried to dissuade him, but he wouldn't listen.

There was quite a large public in the appeal court on the day his appeal was heard.

'Look,' he whispered to me, 'the press is here.'

'So what?'

'Publicity,' he breathed.

'That isn't the sort of publicity you want.'

'Charles, all publicity is good. I'm sure that some film director will come to offer me a contract.'

The only contract poor Figus received was eight months without option in the prison of the Santé. I sent him food parcels, and when he came out he was so pale that I thought he had been taking drugs. Shortly after he took to drugs, and because I disapproved and was even willing to pay for a treatment he vanished completely. Piaf didn't hear from him either.

He reappeared at the time I was on at the Olympia again. He was well dressed, clean and normal. He had acquired a small car.

'Have you inherited money?' I asked.

'Oh no, but the insurance company has at last paid for my accident.'

'Which accident?'

'Yours! The one with the lorry. The money came just in time. I paid my debts, got new suits and this second-hand car.'

'And what did you do with the rest?'

'I spent it on a bathroom for my mother.'

During this period Evelyne and I were divorced and I was a bachelor once more. I have to admit I didn't like it at all.

Dany remained with me as my chauffeur-secretary. He was a great help, and I became devoted to him. I for one can't work with people I am not fond of.

I tried to find consolation in drink and other women's arms, but consolation never comes as easily as that. Finally I fell back on my work.

We went to Brussels, where I had much success. I sang at the Ancienne Belgique, a vast cabaret. The spectators drank during the performance and Dany assured me that the cabaret was full of goodlooking women. Neither the applause nor the sight of the women managed to cheer me up. I felt miserable, and I enjoyed my misery in a fashion. Armenians love suffering.

'The only answer is to have a good time,' said Dany.

As he said that the door of the dressing room opened, and a crowd of young men led by a strikingly tall one burst in. He wasn't interested in Aznavour the singer: he wanted me to become their boon companion for the night. Nothing suited me more in the mood I was.

'It'll do you a lot of good, Charles,' said Dany.

We went from one nightclub to another, champagne, whisky, beer and red wine. By the time we reached the third nightclub Dany and I were rather high. A man came up and suggested a game of dice.

'What's the stake?' I asked.

'Your tie.'

I lost my tie. Another said, 'We'll dice you for your hair.'

'I beg your pardon?'

'If you lose we'll shave your head, if I lose then mine will be shaved.'

I won, and in all that noise and drinking the loser's head was shaved. Then he proposed playing my hair against his eyebrows. I won, and the poor fellow had his eyebrows shaved. He looked like an Oriental idol. Oh, I was enjoying myself! Dany told me to stop dicing, reminding me that I couldn't very well appear next night with my head shaved at the Ancienne Belgique.

Our next stop was a nightclub named Le Boeuf sur le Toit. I was heavy with drink, and sang with the orchestra. Suddenly I had had my fill, in fact more than my fill. All I remembered next morning was my telling Dany I wanted to go home alone, for a lonely man has to be left alone.

In the morning Dany entered the bedroom to wake me up.

'Who's that?' he asked.

'Whom do you mean?'

'The girl beside you.'

I turned my head, and a girl lay beside me, as pretty as you make 'em, yet I hadn't the faintest idea where I had found her, and how she had got into my bed.

'No idea,' I said.

So it went on for a fortnight.

From Brussels we went to Barcelona. By then I had sobered up, and didn't feel like getting drunk any more. Drink doesn't help in the long run, and I realised that I had to choose between my art and drink, for the two don't go hand in hand. Besides, I was on the up and up, and it wasn't the moment to spoil everything. So there was no more drowning my sorrow.

The French artistes who went to Spain always sang in French before their Spanish audiences. I decided I would sing in Spanish as that would appeal far more to the Spaniards. I had some of my chansons translated into Spanish. My sort of chansons were still unknown in Spain, one more reason to let the Spaniards hear them. In Barcelona I sang at the Emporium, a cabaret that employed a number of hostesses. They talk far too much while I sing, I said to myself after the first chanson. I found they talked even more as the night and my singing progressed. I didn't like that, and the next day I saw the manager. I told him I was leaving because I couldn't tolerate the spectators chatting loudly while I sang.

'You're wrong,' said the manager. 'It wasn't the audience talking. We had some American customers, and the hostesses translated your songs from Spanish into English.'

'Tell the hostesses,' I laughed, 'not to translate so loudly.'

Generally French singers remain in Barcelona for two or three performances: I remained a whole week because the people understood what I was singing.

My success in Spain gave me the desire to sing in foreign countries, also to learn foreign languages. I bought a huge map of the world which I studied carefully. Then I called my agent, and said to him, 'There are at least thirty countries where I want to sing.'

'But nobody asks for you,' he said.

'Granted, but I've a little money in the bank, and you can have the lot if you are willing to travel to as many foreign countries as you can and make as much publicity for me as is reasonably possible.'

'Charles, you're mad but I'll do as you want.'

I wished to start in New York since I knew it well owing to my previous visits, and I was beginning to speak English fluently. We went to New York, the year 1964, but we didn't choose the right moment as the newspapers didn't appear because of a printers' strike. So there were no reviews, the papers couldn't speak of me, and that from the financial angle looked disastrous. However, a gentleman called Jack Paar, who had a nightly television programme, never ceased mentioning me during his appearance on the small screen. He spoke in such high praise of me that the theatre where I sang, was full every night. We had feared a flop: the tour turned out to be most profitable.

Then came Italy. I had learnt Italian, later German which for a Frenchman is harder than Spanish or Italian. Slowly foreign parts became more important to me than my native France. Anyhow, it is wrong policy to sing in the same country all the time. If one goes, say, four times a year to the same town it is unlikely that one will find enough spectators for the fourth visit. The public mustn't get accustomed to the same artiste.

I lived in Paris in a room above my parents' flat after my divorce while my house in Galluis was being rebuilt. Aida had come back from Canada. She had divorced too, and back in France she eventually married a young composer called Georges Garvarentz. I was spending more and more time abroad for reasons I have outlined above. I appeared in Lisbon, and on my way back I flew in the same plane as a group of French artistes who had taken part in the Festival of Mar del Plata. So near to the sky I lost my heart to Estelle Blain, a member of the troupe. The attraction was mutual, and once we had landed in Paris we became inseparable. We went out together every night, in short she entered my life completely. At that time too my first serious film, Franjus' *La tête contre les murs* was released. So I had love and fame simultaneously. What more could I want?

My film career was curious indeed. In the beginning—I mean even after I became well known—the film industry wasn't interested in me. Nobody wanted me. When at last Truffaut asked me to make a film with him it came as a surprise. Truffaut believed in me, and the same goes for Cayatte who saw in me the person he needed for his film. But when I started to act in films more regularly the directors discovered they got on well with me. For some unknown reason they had thought the contrary. My films invariably did well. I often think directors sought me out because I am a singer—though I don't sing on the screen—and because they believed I wasn't interested in films.

There may be something in that: perhaps I am more relaxed as an actor because first and foremost I am a singer, so I do not have the same pressures to succeed at this one thing alone. I am not gambling. In any case, I love making films and enjoy working with the people I meet on the set. All my movie career I've heard rude things said about actors and directors and how impossible it is to work with them. I've never found this to be true. I even enjoyed working with Michael Winner in *The Games*. I had to play a runner and I had to win against Michael Crawford. I was 48 or 49 years old and I'd never run in my life. Moreover, it was freezing cold at White City Stadium where we shot that sequence and yet if you see the film, where Michael Crawford looks doubled up because he's trying so desperately to win, both of us were doubled up laughing. By the end of the movie I was almost a good runner.

The film was written by Erich Segal, author of *Love Story* who was a good friend of mine and had always wanted me to play the runner but the producer Richard Zanuck was not convinced, until someone showed him a picture of my legs to see if they could look like a runner's legs. Then, I got the part.

In that film, I met two young actors called Tommy Bergen and Ryan O'Neal. I was always telling Erich Segal that our epoch was a romantic one—and that he should write a romantic love story. He said, 'How can you say that, with all this violence?' I said every revolutionary period has brought out great poets and writers. It's obvious that revolution is a romantic point of view. Later on, he wrote to me and sent me *Love Story*, saying I had been right about romance. I did not think the part was right for me and I recommended Ryan O'Neal.

I've been lucky to work with directors like Réné Clair (*The Devil* and *The Ten Commandments*) and Eli Petrie (*High Fidelity*) and to be starred with beautiful actresses like Claire Bloom, Lesley Caron, Anouk Aimée, Susan Hampshire. Because I am very shy I find it difficult to shoot love scenes 'cold', when I have not even met the person I'm supposed to be making love to. There was excellent rapport between me and Claire Bloom in *High Fidelity*—because she was as shy as me. I wore very thick boxer shorts for the scene in bed and as we were playing two very inhibited people, our shyness came over well on film. In real life, I have to say, my love scenes have generally been outside show business.

English directors I've worked with like Michael Winner and Lewis Gilbert (*The Adventurers, Alfie*) always seem to smoke big cigars and are followed, somehow, by a large box of cigars which seem to materialize when they need it. They also have huge kitchens wherever they go, and the food is terrible!

I love working in Italy, perhaps because I started singing seriously there, and have always been a big success. The Italians think I am Italian which is very gratifying because it is difficult to be a successful singer in a country where everyone is a singer!

In the Piazza San Marco in Venice there are two orchestras and one of them is always playing standards of mine—*Que C'est Triste à Venise*, *The Old-Fashioned Way*, *La Bohème*, *L'Istrione* and *Yesterday When I was Young*.

My brother-in-law Georges Garvarentz went to Italy and did scores for many important movies there. We worked together on *Taxi to Tobruk* and many others.

When I play in a film I do it naturally, that is to say I act as I feel I should. I don't prepare myself for it. I play the part I have been given to the best of my ability, but I don't study my part for months, or try to live the part. I act instinctively because I sing instinctively. When directors feel that a part is difficult to play on the screen they come to me as they know I am not afraid and that I will do my best. They have seldom been wrong, and as it happens my name does seem to draw the cinema public.

Truffaut, like so many other French film directors, wanted to make films with plenty of music and singing. He wished to make a documentary about me as he was fascinated by the music-hall. I was willing and I said so, but then I didn't hear from him for a time. Suddenly, he telephoned, asking me to see him.

'I've found a book by an American author which I like immensely. We'll make a film of it and it'll take the place of the documentary.'

Thus *Tirez sur le Pianist*, *Shoot the Piano Player*, was born.

When Truffaut wrote the screenplay of *À bout de Souffle*, *Breathless*, he took Jean-Luc Godard as director. Godard thought that I was the right actor for the leading part. He came to see me, I read the screenplay and I immediately saw that the part wasn't for me. I said so. After my refusal he engaged another actor for the part whose name was Belmondo, and whom the part suited admirably. Thus began Belmondo's meteoric career. I was right in every sense when I said the part wasn't for me.

The most difficult thing for me to do was to play the part of Charles Aznavour in *Une Gosse Sensas*. Should I be modest, and if not, would people think I was too sure of myself, too boastful? I had the same difficulty with *Paris Music-Hall*, but somehow I did find the golden middle way in both films.

All that takes me a long way from Estelle Blain, though not altogether because I acted with her in a film entitled *Les Dragueurs*. And it was the cinema that brought about the end of our great passion. Our roads parted because her career as a film actress came for her before me or anybody else. But it was great while it lasted.

Chapter Thirteen

Piaf died in 1963 at the age of forty-eight. The last time I saw her she was already extremely ill. She had sent for me, and I went to see her in the nursing home she would never leave alive. She died a few days later. Just before her death she wanted to see me again, but as she was in the South of France and I in Paris it was too late to get to her. Her body was brought back to Paris for burial.

There was such a crowd at the funeral that some of the distinguished mourners were pushed into the open grave. People took photographs, and asked the celebrities who had come to pay their last respects to Piaf for their autographs. I could almost hear Piaf saying to me, 'Do you see this huge crowd? Do you think you'll have as many at your burial?'

Sarapo, her last lover, was a really lovely, sincere fellow. He was completely broken up by her death and I went back to Piaf's house after the funeral and tried to help him. Later, he was killed in a car crash. He had always been afraid of cars.

Piaf had been a star in every sense, a lasting star, with all the qualities and faults of a great star.

When I am asked when I began to consider myself a star I can't give a direct answer. By 1964 I could call myself a star in France, Belgium, Switzerland and North Africa, and even in the Lebanon. Where other artistes were engaged for a fortnight at the most I was offered contracts for six weeks. In Marseilles the usual run was three days: I remained for a month. In Brussels others sang for one week, I for three weeks, and so on. One can begin to look on oneself as a star when one is engaged for longer periods than others are, and when one feels at the end of a chanson that one has never sung better before, that is to say if the applause warrants that feeling.

Shortly after Estelle and I had parted I decided to go on tour all on my own in the French provinces. My reasons, as explained to Dany, were simple and logical. I would try out several new chansons, and make some money.

'You're the boss,' said Dany without any enthusiasm.

His scepticism annoyed me a little. Surely I knew what I was doing. I got my troupe together, hired musicians and bought a small bus, the lot paid out of my own pocket as it was to be my own venture.

We opened in Marseilles. Immediately after our arrival in the town I was assailed by autograph hunters, most of them women.

'A good sign,' I said to Dany who just grunted.

I was staying in a five-star hotel on the Canebière, the right abode for a star of the chanson. I spent my first afternoon working on a new song, the dictionary of rhymes at my side. Then I went to the theatre, arriving in my dressing room early as is my wont because I need peace and quiet to be able to concentrate before my appearance on the stage. Despite the peace and quiet I need I love listening to the sounds of the theatre coming to life.

'All seats are booked,' Dany announced.

That reassured me, for I had sold almost everything I possessed and even took a mortgage on my house, to finance the tour. As it wasn't enough Breton had to lend me some money.

I went on stage, sang to the best of my ability, and received an ovation that only a warmhearted town like

Marseilles can give. Back in my dressing room I received scores of admirers. Dany whispered in my ear that an enormous crowd had assembled outside the stage door, and hundreds of voices were shouting my name. I would be torn to pieces by the fans, mostly young girls, if I went out. What were we to do?

I found the answer. I told Dany to ask the police to take me back to the hotel in a black maria.

'But that's never been done,' protested Dany.

'Let this be the first time it's done,' I said.

I knew my Marseillais. If they don't care for you they ignore you; if they do they practically kill you while trying to show you how much they love and admire you. They want to hug you, every one of them.

When I came out through the stage door the black maria was waiting for me with a row of policemen on each side of it. I had only five steps to take to reach haven.

'Hurry,' called Dany.

It was too late. The crowd had seen me, pushed forward, sweeping the policemen off their feet, and fell on me. There is no other way of describing it. They tore off my tie, tousled my hair, stamped on my feet, tore off my buttons. I lost a shoe and when I lifted my head I received an elbow in the eye. I was gasping like a drowning man. A policeman who was inside the black maria got hold of my hand, and pulled me towards him. In the end I found myself on my knees inside the black maria, my suit torn, my lips bleeding, my eye swelling. Moreover, I had lost Dany in the enthusiastic crowd. The black maria forced its way through the crowd while I sat on the floor, resembling a tramp who had been picked up by the police in a disreputable fight more than the successful star of the evening.

I got into a hot bath the moment I reached the hotel. Dany didn't look too good either when he got back at last.

'If it's like this every night,' I said, 'we won't return to Paris alive.'

Unfortunately it wasn't like that every night and I often wished during the tour that I was back in the turbulent crowds of Marseilles. The Bordeaux theatre had two thousand five hundred seats; only eight hundred spectators turned up. In Anjou and Brittany I sang to empty houses. There were still forty towns to visit with my troupe.

'Cancel it,' said Dany.

'I can't do that. I can't let down the other members of the troupe.'

'Others have done it without bothering about the troupe.'

'I just couldn't.'

Bad luck that amounted to disaster pursued us from town to town. My friends and colleagues did their best to console me.

'It's the end of the month, people are short of money.'

'We had the wrong sort of publicity.'

'They don't listen to the radio in this part of the country, so they don't know how famous you are.'

'The previous troupe that came here was so bad that the local people got so disgusted that they don't want to go to the theatre any more.'

The reasons my friends gave hid the real cause of our failure. I had overestimated my strength and fame, and I should have left the bookings to an agent. I swore never to repeat my two mistakes again. In the meantime I was losing millions of old francs on that tour. It would take me years to strike even again. On the other hand, my debts spurred me to write and work harder.

The tour continued, and I sang to empty seats. My failure, I thought, should be turned into victory in time. I improved my repertoire of songs, in fact assembled the chansons I would sing on my return to Paris. It became a foolproof repertoire. I arrived in Paris with empty pockets but completely sure of myself.

My voice was worrying me again. Would my veiled, rough, hoarse voice last through the years stretching in front of me? Now and then my voice was strong, but generally it didn't live up to my expectations. It often gave the impression that a piece of Gruyère cheese with its many holes was wedged in my throat. And never had I needed my voice more. I was engaged to sing at the Alhambra in Paris, and to succeed at the Alhambra was in many ways the crowning of a singer's career. (The Alhambra doesn't exist any more.) I was looking forward to the Alhambra and feared it at the same time. Of one thing I was certain, namely that my whole career depended on the public's and the press's reaction on the opening night at the Alhambra.

A few days before the fateful night I went to see a throat specialist.

'One of your vocal cords,' he said after he had examined me, 'isn't developed, that is isn't strong enough. All your troubles are caused by that cord.'

'Can one do anything about it?'

'Nothing whatsoever.'

'Could one operate on it?'

'That would be a waste of time since there's nothing abnormal about your vocal cords. So many other people have a cord that isn't strong enough.'

'What do they do?'

'They don't sing.'

I paid the specialist, and went to see a well known singing teacher. After the third lesson he observed, 'I taught you to breathe in a new fashion. You won't tire your vocal cords too much if you breathe like that. I can't do any more for you. In your place I'd choose a different profession.'

I related to father what the specialist and teacher had said. Father had a strong voice which he could fully use even after he had dined and drunk copiously.

'I'd give a lot to be able to give you my voice,' he said.

Thinking it over I reached the conclusion that taking it all in all mine was the voice of my own generation, not strong enough to proclaim lasting truths, but with the right timbre to sing of nights of love. In any case it was the appropriate voice for the chansons I wrote. After those two visits I decided not to bother about my voice any more. Besides, I had no alternative.

For my first night at the Alhambra I brought my own loudspeaker material. I put two loudspeakers behind me on the stage. I would tire my voice less like that.

When the rehearsal started I took possession of my dressing room. I find it of immense importance to feel at home in a dressing room, especially if I am going to spend a considerable time in it.

'Bring me a screen,' I ordered. 'The sight of the wash basin makes me sick. It's a revolting sight.'

I overheard a stage hand muttering, 'What will he be like when he becomes really famous?'

I arrived early at the Alhambra on my first night, sat down in the dressing room and the nervewrecking waiting began. I tried to look calm, serene, even jovial, yet I chainsmoked all the time. I checked on everything: my stage suit, shirt, the whale bones of my collar, socks and shoes. Oh my God! I had forgotten the cuff links. I called in everybody who was within earshot. Could any of them lend me his cuff links? Then I noticed that they were already in the buttonholes. Stage fever is a rotten disease.

'I'm going out to eat a sandwich,' I called. 'If anyone asks for me say I'll be back in a jiffy.'

It wasn't a matter of nerves: it was plain fear. I trotted to the nearest bistro, where I asked for a sandwich. In the bad old days when all I could afford was a sandwich I dreamed of copious repasts. Now that I could afford such repasts I only found time to eat a sandwich. As a matter of fact, I left half the sandwich uneaten, I was in such a hurry to get back to the Alhambra.

'Are you all right?' the waiter asked in the bistro.

'I'll be all right tomorrow.'

For tomorrow I would either be an acclaimed star or a flop deserving oblivion. The Alhambra would be the turning point of my career for better or worse.

Two press photographers were waiting for me at the

theatre. A journalist accompanied the photographers. Though I hadn't seen him before he immediately addressed me by my Christian name. I didn't know how to take that. Was it a form of condescension or the contrary? I was too nervous to decide.

'Behave as if we weren't here,' said one of the photographers.

He pushed the screen aside and climbed on the washbasin which nearly collapsed under his weight. His colleague lay down flat on the floor after having kicked my guitar.

'Like this,' he explained, 'we won't photograph you from the same angle.'

'Do whatever you want,' I said, 'but frankly, you don't look very natural in your postures.'

That made everybody laugh. Later they took me outside to photograph me in front of the enormous bill that carried my name. When the photographers had had their fill they hurried off to the café leaving me alone with the journalist who asked me why I always worked so hard. He had been told I toiled like a slave.

'Honestly, I don't know why I work so hard,' I answered. 'It must be a physical and moral necessity with me. If I work I know I exist and I know too that some day, which I pray is very far away, I will have all the time in the world to rest.'

'Where?'

'In eternity.'

Before we parted outside the stage door the journalist asked me to speak about my luck.

'My luck was that I never had any luck. My only trump card was that I looked like everybody else, the man in the street, the man with whom anybody can identify himself. I am often told that I look like thousands of others. That doesn't shock me. As a matter of fact, it amuses me.'

'Good luck, Charles,' said the journalist, and left me all alone in the dressing room. It was only seven in the evening, two more hours to kill before my fate was decided upon. While I fretted and waited my thoughts went back to Piaf who had said in my unknown days that the chansons I had written for others would in time be sung by me before vast audiences, and they would have a greater success than they used to have with other singers.

Dany appeared in the dressing room, and gave me the ignition key of my South Sea blue Thunderbolt. I got into the car, and drove to my parents to embrace them and my daughter Patricia. I stayed with them for nearly an hour. When I got back to the Alhambra my staunch friends and admirers were waiting in the dressing room—Jean-Louis Marquet, Vernon, Figus, Androu Ehka, Aida and Garvarentz. On the table lay many telegrams, and a fresh one arrived every minute or so. They were from the Compagnons de la Chanson, Montand, Signoret, the Bretons, Jacqueline François, Jean Cocteau, Marcel Achard, Charles Trenet, and umpteen others, as if the whole postal service were put at my disposal.

Suddenly the orchestra began to play the introduction to the first part of the programme. Fear grabbed me again, my throat was dry, and my heart thumped. I glanced at my reflection in the mirror: I looked green. I spread a lot of stage make-up over my cheeks, for none should guess the state I was in. I dressed hurriedly for the stage. It took me five efforts to tie my tie properly. By then it was the interval.

Breton came into the dressing room. He was the only person allowed in next to Dany.

'How do you feel?' he asked.

'Ready to be devoured.'

'You should bite first.'

'I fear my teeth aren't strong enough.'

'It's either they or you. Choose, old man.'

I went on stage, feeling as if the end had come. Nobody had to announce me as I was the star of the performance. The orchestra was conducted by Jean Leccia. I looked at the people in the first row: they appeared to me hostile.

My turn had come, there was no backing out any more. I stepped forward, and was blinded by the lights. I was received with polite applause, not much of an encouragement. The mike wasn't high enough, and while I adjusted it I noticed that my hands were wet. I was choking, and I couldn't imagine a sound escaping from my open mouth. You longed to be here, I said to myself. Now you're here, so let them hear you, you foolish Armenian! I saw a fly, I nearly swallowed it. Then at last the sounds came, and I heard my voice singing a chanson of mine. I couldn't make out anybody, I beheld only an immense dark hole, and that dark hole was the *Tout-Paris* that can make or unmake you according to its whim. My voice I thought was flat, and my right leg trembled. In that state I sang four chansons, and when I reached the fifth I had the impression that I was singing to a non-existent audience. I received applause from the gallery, where my own fans were assembled. At the sixth chanson I was convinced that the battle was lost. My shirt was wet, so hard was I sweating. All my hope now rested on the seventh song, *Je me voyais déjà*. I went to change which I did rapidly, then I was back, and sang that song.

There was frightening silence when I had finished *Je me voyais déjà*. Then I heard the fateful noise of the spectators rising, ready to leave. I am lost because I lost, I said to myself. And at that very moment the whole audience burst into thunderous applause. They had remained cold and inimical during six chansons, but the seventh overwhelmed them. In a sense I won after I had thrown in the sponge. There we were facing one another, I the solitary singer and the capricious first night audience. They had given in, not I.

The curtain dropped, then it rose, and I was back on stage to finish my repertoire of songs. My victory was complete, and I could say after that night that my career would never be in danger again. While I received in the dressing room the congratulations of my wellwishers and admirers I thought of my struggles, frustrated hopes and humiliations that were the foundation stone of my career.

Chapter Fourteen

As I have said before, Maurice Chevalier had been a staunch supporter of mine from the beginning of my struggles. Yet we hadn't very much in common as human beings. I am an open person, whereas Chevalier was a secretive man. I like to see old and new faces around me: Chevalier didn't care for people walking into his life. He was, I could say, in every sense the contrary of Piaf who loved mankind. I have told the story of our first meeting earlier in this book, but it is worth repeating because it shows the conscientious, almost pedantic person he was. I met him, that is saw him in the metro during the war when the metro was practically the only means of transport in Paris. I gave him one of my chansons—one of those early ones—and I said I had written it and should like him to sing it. He took it, and I didn't hear from him again, I mean not for the next twenty years. When we met after that long interval it transpired that I had forgotten to put my address on the music sheet, thus it was impossible for him to get in touch with me. It would never have occurred to him to use it without the author's consent.

A good example of Chevalier's secretive nature was a visit I paid him with Roche to show him one of our chansons. He told me to leave the room because he didn't want me to see him trying the chanson out, that is how to approach it, the gestures it needed, and the way he would finally decide to sing it. Roche remained in the room to accompany him on the piano. Chevalier told him to sit down at the piano but not to turn round while he worked. He was not allowed to see how the great Maurice did his tricks, either. As a matter of fact, he didn't take the chanson.

Chevalier met me some time later, and said, 'You'll have to do something about that song. What about changing the words?'

'No, thank you. I never change the words of my chansons.'

'But there are things one just can't say in chansons.'

'Soon everybody will start saying them, so I don't want to be left out or behind.'

'If you're so pretentious,' said Chevalier, 'you'll never get anywhere.'

He said that in a very friendly manner.

'If using the words one believes in is pretentious,' I said, 'I prefer to be considered pretentious. I don't want to change the meaning of any of my chansons. If you take it as it is I'll be happy, but if you don't like it as it is—well, then you won't sing it.'

After that we didn't see each other for a considerable time.

The next time I saw him was while I sang Chez Patachou. By then the chanson had changed, and was approaching my way of looking at it. However, Chevalier still refused to accept the new fashion. He was a stubborn man. Besides it wasn't for his generation. Paradoxically that made our relationship easier, for now it was one generation speaking to the other. Moreover, he had learnt that nobody likes being told how to write chansons and how to sing them. In short, he had stopped giving me lessons. It shouldn't be overlooked that ten years had elapsed between my working with Roche and singing Chez Patachou, and in the meantime he had become aware of my chansons not doing too badly, and that my lyrics weren't as preposterous as he had thought. Henceforth the only advice he gave me was how to place my chansons. He knew his trade too well to underestimate my work.

When I toured America for the fourth time on my own, and I reached Hollywood I found he was in town. In fact, it was he who came to see me to ask me whether I would care for him to announce me on the stage of my first appearance. Of course, I jumped at it since his name was legendary in Hollywood. And truly he appeared on stage, and this is how he announced me:

'I want to introduce a young Frenchman. He has a great deal of talent, I'd like him to be my son. Mind you, I'd prefer him to be my brother, and to speak frankly nothing would please me more than having him as my father.'

I thanked him, and in order to show my gratitude I wrote a song entitled *Môme de mon quartier* for him. I wrote it after I got back to Paris.

He came to see me, and I said, 'Maurice, I wrote a love song for you.'

'I don't sing love songs any more,' he said. 'At my age it's too late for love songs.'

'But my love song is a song of love to all the women of your past, not one in particular, but to the lot of them.'

He asked me to play it. He was deeply moved because nobody thought of writing songs for him any more. Tears appeared in his eyes while I played the chanson, and when I gave it to him he sobbed loudly. From that day onward we were truly intimate friends, though with him there were always reservations. He used his age as a barrier. He didn't let people who were much younger than he enter his intimacy too much.

He was always punctual. If he made a date with you he arrived at the exact minute. If he asked me to his apartment for eight o'clock sharp I was expected to be at the door at five to eight, as the door would open precisely at eight sharp.

On one occasion I invited both him and Fernandel to dinner. I enjoyed having those two sacred monsters in my company. If one belongs to that world it is important to become acquainted with the great ones of that world. I had invited them to a famous and expensive restaurant. I was perfectly aware that they were both cagey with money, and neither of them believed in lavishness. I intended to show them that I for one did believe in it. We were all of us in Venice, and Chevalier was staying at the Hotel Splendide if I remember rightly. He asked me to fetch him at eight o'clock in the evening. I arrived at the hotel a few seconds before eight: at eight sharp the lift door opened and Chevalier emerged from the lift. He looked at his wrist watch, then at me, and said, 'Perfect.'

That dinner was like a display of fireworks. I am not good at talking about my past, but those two talked about theirs with verve and gusto. The extraordinary thing about them was that Fernandel had started as a singer, and left the chanson for the cinema never to return to the chanson, whereas Chevalier who had gone from the chanson to the films returned to the chanson despite the immense success of his films. It was an unforgettable evening with four different generations at the table: Chevalier, Fernandel, myself and Marius, Fernandel's son.

Chevalier was never surprised and marvelled at nothing. But Fernandel marvelled at everything and loved surprise. To sit beside Chevalier was a cause for marvel with Fernandel. Much older and more famous: how marvellous! Not that Fernandel suffered from undue modesty, but he had respect for people of achievement without forgetting his own achievements. His amazingly childlike eyes could fill with wonder and astonishment which gave him his special strength as a film actor. So the dinner in Venice was a great success, especially as it was I who paid for it.

It is no secret that Chevalier didn't like spending money, and the same went for Fernandel. They both said so quite openly.

I went once to see Fernandel in Paris to discuss a film idea. He offered me a Pernod, saying 'Take as much as you want. I get it free from a friend.'

He was given an American car as a present. 'What, no automatic windows?' he exclaimed as he examined the present. The car was sent back to America to be fitted with electric windows, naturally at the expense of the man who had made him the gift. Alas, the days of such expensive presents are over! Alas again, I came too late on the scene.

Jean Cocteau was one of the great people I truly admired, and his friendship was a most precious one. Before he came to see me for the first time I had quickly read all his work, but it wasn't a good edition of his work. When I told him that he sent me all his books in an excellent edition, each volume inscribed by him. From time to time he wrote me delightful, short letters, and we often met in the house of some mutual friends. When I sang in the Casino in Beaulieu-sur-Mer he came regularly to hear me sing.

Cocteau loved people who were younger than he, and believed in youth and all youth stood for. He always gave very good advice. I had read little before I met him, but had read everything he wrote because I felt he wrote for my generation. Beside Cocteau I think I had only read Victor Hugo. However, I did admire writers, and I did want to improve my education that had stopped at the age of ten. I asked Cocteau to make me a list of the twenty-five books he found the most important in world literature. He made the list, I read every one of the books he recommended, and how I wish I hadn't lost that list. Otherwise I would reproduce it here.

Cocteau was a strong believer in personal discipline. He sat down to write every day at the same time. I asked him once, 'Of course when you sit down to write it is to write one of your books.'

'Oh no,' he answered. 'I write because I don't want to lose the habit of writing. I write every day even when I have nothing to say, just to keep myself in training. You ought to write every day too.'

I took his advice. Since then I write every day, perhaps four lines, maybe ten lines without bothering whether I will use them or not. And it is very useful, for when I have a good idea I can put it to paper in a more compact and clear form because of my habit of writing every day.

When Cocteau made his film *Le Testament d'Orphée* he wanted all his friends to appear in it.

'But there's no part for me in it,' I said.

'Just appear in the film for a moment like an extra. Let your face be seen. I repeat, I want all my friends in it.'

One of the most important things that happened to me before my present—and best—marriage, was my meeting with Liza Minnelli. I met her at a party in New York and I was totally lost at that party. I'm always lost at parties, especially in foreign countries and I always ask myself what am I doing here in spite of the fact that this was a party being given for me by a friend of the girl I was in love with at the time—a girl called Isabelle. I remember that Bette Davis was there and that she had just returned from England and was going around saying 'those young English actresses are all fantastic.'

Liza was very young—about seventeen, and I'd just seen her in the *Johnny Carson Show* and I'd talked to my brother-in-law about her, and we'd both said she was not only talented, she was also built like a goddess.

Well, she opened her big eyes at me and said. 'Gee, I saw you the other day, you were great.'

After New York I went to Los Angeles and she was singing there at the Coconut Grove. After her show I went to see her to tell her she was very good and also that there were some things I didn't like. To give her some honest criticism, in fact. She took it very well, and I went back and wrote her a letter in my special English and before I caught the plane I sent her roses. I asked her if she wanted to join me in Montreal where I was appearing next.

She came to Montreal, and what had to happen happened. We had a wonderful, crazy time together. She was young and had enough energy and *joie de vivre* to make anything happen. She could do everything—dance, sing, act. She was crazy enough to tapdance with my secretary and to dance and sing through the streets of the city with me, and yet at the same time she was worried about whether she would be a success. It was a difficult time for her. I was sure she would be a success and I told her so.

At that time, Liza had made one record, but I told her she would be a star without any records. I wanted to introduce her to the French public—the most difficult and the best public in the world because you have to win them over.

I am a man who always wants to marry when I am in love and I wondered whether to ask her to marry me. We were very much in love. She took my shirt and she still wears it. It was very much against my belief to marry someone in showbusiness—even someone who had enough talent to succeed. One of our personalities would have to be crushed and both of us were too strong to allow it.

I then went to Las Vegas to hear her. She told me a lot about her mother, Judy Garland, and how even a strong personality like hers had to survive being crushed.

What happened between Liza and me was more than friendship and less than love. Love doesn't think, and I had to think. We had enormous conversations about showbiz and our approach to it. My best listener has always been Liza. Each time I see her I see my influence on her. She is a little like Piaf in some ways. She is a lost girl too and she has the giant personality and the *joie de vivre*. The only one who could play Piaf in a film would be Liza. She's a warrior and will stay at the top for a long time.

We talked and talked about singing and love right through the nights, but I knew we could not have had the kind of quiet, family life I yearned for. She is too much of a star and it is better to have a beautiful friendship like the one we have than a failed marriage.

She sings my songs nowadays, and she sings them *beautifully*.

My friends included Ted Lapidus of whom I have spoken before, and whom I had met on the same day as my second wife. Lapidus and I had a lot in common. We were both Frenchmen, yet both of us were sons of immigrants. His

parents were Jewish, mine Armenians, and both of us made
our names, I in the chanson, he in dressmaking. We understand each other perfectly as his is an artistic disposition
too, and he writes charming poems. We discuss the same
sort of subjects, now and then even after a three months
interval. One of our favourite subjects is religion. He belongs
to the Jewish faith, I to the Armenian Church, nonetheless
we see eye to eye on matters of religion. We frequently
spent our holidays together.

He was a great chaser of skirts; I slightly less. I love
women as much as he, but with me it is living with
a woman that matters most. To my mind living with a
woman gives the man complete freedom, whereas running
after women is akin to slavery. When you chase after
women you never know how it will end. A chance encounter
might end up with her moving in with you, eventually
forcing you to get out of your own home in order to
be rid of her. However, if the woman is of your own
choice, living with her gives you the liberty of leading
your own life.

Lapidus and I were on holiday in Saint-Tropez. Lapidus
had a Danish woman friend whose bosom friend was a
Swedish girl. The Swedish girl was called Ulla, and I had
met her with Lapidus in Paris for an instant. I caught
sight of her in Saint-Tropez shortly after my arrival. We
sat at a table, Sacha Distel, Ted Lapidus, Régine and I.
Ours was really a table of stars as Bardot was with us
too. The night before I had said to Régine that I was
sick and tired of my bachelor's existence. I hated going
out, yet I was forced to go out if I wanted to pick up
a girl. If only I could find the right girl I would marry
her at once.

Régine must have remembered our chat of last night
because she suddenly said, 'Look, that's the sort of girl
you should marry.'

I looked, and there was Ulla going past the café. I
jumped up, and went to fetch her. She had just arrived
from Sweden, and didn't know any of the famous people

present. She thought I was probably the son of a rich businessman. I asked her to dance, she said she didn't dance. I said I should love to see her again. Perhaps was the answer.

But as Saint-Tropez is small we ran into each other several times. Then she had to leave for Paris, where she worked in a bank. In Saint-Tropez she hadn't been keen on having an affair with a singer. She thought that singers didn't earn much money, and weren't interesting people to know. She looked at everybody and everything from a Swedish angle, and Sweden is a very small country. Nevertheless, she came to live with me in the end, but when I went on an American tour—I wasn't thinking of marriage yet—she returned to her parents in Sweden. Anyhow, it was against her principles to live with a man without being married to him. Our living together hadn't pleased her strict Protestant parents either. Suddenly I saw the light. Ulla was in every possible way the ideal wife for me.

I telephoned her in Kalmar, where she was living at the time.

'If you want to marry me then come. I'm in Las Vegas, and we can get married when you arrive.'

She packed a suitcase, and flew to Las Vegas. I called my sister, my new brother-in-law and my daughter to tell them I was getting married. Unfortunately, I couldn't call my mother because she had died recently, but she had met Ulla, and Aida reminded me she had liked her a lot.

When I say Ulla flew to Las Vegas I should add that she stopped in Paris on her way for Lapidus to make her wedding dress. We got married shortly after her arrival. That was in January 1967. A year later we were married in the Armenian Church in Paris. That was my second wedding in that church. The priest said when I had informed him that I wished to marry again, 'My son, one can't be married a second time in the Armenian Church, but we'll make an exception with you.'

'Father, I couldn't marry anywhere else.'

'All right, but let this be really the last time.'

This is, without doubt, my best and quietest marriage. Ulla

does not interfere in any way with my work, nor does she pretend to know anything about it. We have three beautiful children, Katya, Misha and Nicholas and I shall not mind at all if they go on the stage. Katya already knows at nine years old, which of my new songs she likes and which she doesn't. She goes around humming the ones she likes.

I help in the house when I am at home and play as domestic a role as possible. I reckon I was very lucky in my own family life and I want my children to be as warmly understood as I was.

By that time my dear and faithful friend Raoul Breton had left this earth, where he had done so much good. I still mourn him, and when he died suddenly I was unable to do any work for weeks. The music publishing house of Raoul Breton was the achievement of a couple, his and his wife's. She carried on after his death in the same spirit as in his lifetime. Without his friendship and encouragement I couldn't have achieved my aim in life. In many ways it was he who made me. Not a day goes by without my thinking of him and all he has done for me. His widow and I have remained close friends, and I often go to see her.

I travelled wider and wider in pursuit of my successful career. In 1961 I had gone to Russia, and when I arrived there I felt like the native returning to his country. Wasn't I the son of my father? My progress in Russia was triumphal in every sense. I believe I became the best known foreign artiste in the Soviet Union. But it wasn't like this at the beginning of my tour. In Moscow they allocated me the Theatre of the Strada, which specialised in variety shows. I am an accommodating person; however, I considered a variety theatre beneath the dignity of the singer I am. I insisted on singing in a concert hall with the result that they gave me the Tchaikovski Theatre to sing in. After that I had no more trouble with them.

Naturally, the most exciting and important days of my Russian tour was my visit to Armenia, the country of my roots. It snowed heavily on the day I arrived, and I was told it hadn't snowed like that for seventy-five years. The Emperor of All the Russians had been to Armenia on that day of heavy snow seventy-five years ago. He wanted to see Mount Ararat, but because of the snow it was impossible to get near the mountain. The Emperor said to the mountain, 'Mount Ararat, I was unable to see you, but you haven't seen me either.'

I find that a rather stupid remark and when it was repeated to me I couldn't help observing, 'Well, Mount Ararat hasn't seen me either.'

I stayed in Armenia for four days. I made the acquaintance of my paternal grandmother who was ninety-six years old. At the airport about two hundred and fifty people waited for me, and when they caught sight of me they all burst into tears. I was astonished, just couldn't make out why they should cry. After all they had never seen me before. One of my many aunts said, 'You look so cold, little one.' We were speaking in Armenian.

'Yes, I'm cold, but why do you people cry?'

'Because you're here and because we've never seen you before.'

'You cry because I'm well known. You wouldn't have a tear for me if I were unknown.'

They were a bit annoyed, nonetheless my four days stay went off very well. I was to sing in the local Opera House, their largest theatre. They gave me a piano for my work, not a bad piano, but there was a Steinway in the same room. 'Why don't you let me use the Steinway?' I asked.

'The Steinway is for concerts,' was the reply.

'It's for me,' I said. 'You either give it or I won't sing.'

I was given the Steinway. I believe they let me play on it because I spoke Armenian as well as they.

I discovered that the best seats were reserved for the local high officials. As a result of that the students chalked on the wall, 'The seats are for the officials, but Aznavour is for us.' There were no seats for my relations either.

'I'm not going to sing,' I told the officials, 'if there aren't seven seats reserved for my relations every night.'

'In that case we'll put in some extra chairs,' they said.

I saw to my grandmother sitting in the front row every night. At each performance I was to hand a handkerchief to the spectators. It was my grandmother who received it each time.

I met all my many relations, and while I took a meal with them one of my uncles said, 'You came with five musicians. How many musicians are you allowed in France?'

'Allowed? What do you mean by allowed? I engage as many musicians as I want. The last time at the Olympia I had fifty-five musicians.'

'Impossible,' said the uncle.

'Impossible? What do you mean when you say impossible?'

'They wouldn't let you have so many musicians.'

I became angry which I regretted afterwards. It wasn't the uncle's fault that he didn't understand what life is like in non-communist countries. But while my anger lasted I couldn't resist saying to him, 'If I want three thousand musicians I've every right to employ them even if there are only three spectators in the theatre.'

'That's a lie,' he shouted.

'How dare you call me a liar?'

'Because what you say is impossible. Here . . .'

'Here,' I interrupted, 'I wouldn't even have a car. There I have a Rolls-Royce.'

We shouted at each other, but when we rose from the table I calmed down, realising that it was just a waste of breath trying to explain the Western way of life.

During my stay in Armenia I paid a call on the Head of the Armenian Church. The Armenian religion became the state religion of Armenia in the third century, the first Christian state religion in the world. I was accompanied to that meeting by the whole French communist press. The Head of the Church is known as the Catholicos.

'You're not married, my son,' he said. I wasn't at the time.

'In my profession as in yours, Father,' I replied, 'Marriage isn't very important.'

I made him laugh which didn't please him in the long run since laughter destroys dignity. The Armenian Church is like the Armenian language. They are both completely on their own. The Armenian language resembles no other language, and the Armenian Church isn't like any other church.

Speaking of my travels, I visit foreign countries only in the course of my work, and I work, that is sing all over the world. There are few countries I haven't been to. According to my point of view a conscientious singer should make no exceptions. Shall I be better paid in this country or that one? That sort of reasoning doesn't enter my mind. If they can pay well let them pay well; if they can't I am not going to turn my back on them. I have no fixed price, my price depends on the town or country I sing in. I am not like some of my colleagues who say a hundred performances a year should bring in so much, as that is the sum I need for the year. I don't look at it like that, for there are many countries that can't afford to pay a high price.

When I go to Mexico—I often go to Mexico—I even sing in a square or a market place because I know that local people simply can't afford to pay for theatre or concert tickets. On the other hand, where they can afford it they have to pay the price.

I love wandering round in an unknown country, or even in a familiar country, in order to understand the people better. I love visiting cathedrals and the old parts of the towns, but watching the people in the streets gives me twice as much pleasure. When I take photographs I prefer people to old buildings.

Japan is one of the countries I like best. I, who am a short European, find all the discomfort of a tall man when I go to Japan. The cloakrooms are too low, the

186

hotel rooms too small. In short, I feel tall in Japan. In Japanese hotel bedrooms I can't help wondering whether the washbasin is a chamber pot or not, so low it invariably is.

One day in Japan I wanted to buy a jacket with a lot of pockets. I never seem to have enough pockets. I said to the Japanese shop assistant: 'I want a jacket, small size.'

He looked me up and down, then said, 'No large size.'

'No, I want it small size.'

He stared at me astonished, then said, 'But you're very tall.'

For them I was. So I bought a large size jacket which was just the right size for me. I was accompanied by a friend who is shorter than I. He turned to my assistant, and said in a proud voice, 'Large size for me too.'

'No, no,' said the Japanese. 'Medium size.'

I had resolved already in my days of struggle not to visit England before I had acquainted myself with the United States. In those days America seemed nearer to a French artiste than the United Kingdom. And it seemed easier to get there. Moreover, I wanted to be able to speak fluent English before I crossed the Channel. I enjoy listening to an Englishman speaking English. The American audiences have many advantages: they are good humoured, always ready to acclaim you. They want to enjoy themselves, and if you succeed in making them enjoy themselves the battle is won. An English audience is far more critical. In that respect the English resemble the French.

After my several American tours an impresario offered me a contract to sing in London. He suggested the Prince of Wales Theatre which I happened to know in that I had gone to London some time before for the special reason of breaking off my love affair with a young actress who was performing at that theatre. I had gone to London just to tell her that it was finished between her and me.

That, I repeat, is how I came to know the Prince of Wales Theatre. But England I didn't know at all since I hadn't been there before, and left it on the same day I broke up with the girl.

I said no to the impresario when he mentioned the Prince of Wales Theatre.

'Then where do you want to sing?' he asked.

'I don't know, but I'm willing to go to London to have a look round at the different theatres.'

He agreed, and we set out for London. I was still completely unknown in England. We looked at different theatres and concert halls. When we got to the Albert Hall I said, 'This is where I'd like to sing.'

'You're mad,' cried the impresario. 'It's far too vast. Seven thousand seats!'

I told him that with a few extra curtains I could manage perfectly well in the Albert Hall. Its very size suited me in every respect. I feel far more at home in a large theatre or concert hall than in a small one. The agent did as I bade him though he couldn't believe that the hitherto unknown Charles Aznavour could fill the Albert Hall. Every ticket was sold. That was in 1967.

In the beginning in America I had to read the English versions of my chansons before the audiences. By the time I started my singing career in England my English was fluent enough to sing in English without any aid. When I was asked in England why I had waited such a long time to come and sing in Britain my answer was that England had always seemed far away to me, at an immense distance from France. In England I found that to most English people France appeared just as far away.

Perhaps English came more naturally to me than to most French artistes because I had deep admiration for the English music hall which I knew well. Even when I didn't speak English I was aware of the existence and work of all their famous music hall stars.

In every country the singer has to address the public in a slightly different way. I quickly learnt how to address a British audience.

I travelled all over England several times. I love spending many hours in small towns and villages, drinking tea and eating scones. I am a keen collector of antiques, which is an added reason to visit the towns in the countries I sing in. Now England is a paradise for collectors of antiques. As the years and my visits to England accumulate I feel more and more at home in that country that had once seemed so frighteningly distant.

When I am on tour and stay in a town longer than a day I hire a piano because I never cease working while I travel. My chief reason for working so hard when I am on tour is to be able to spend as much time as I can with Ulla and my children when I get home. If there isn't time to hire a piano I use my little electric piano which always accompanies me. After the performance I usually return to the hotel to lie down. The great days of staying out most of the night are over. Besides, my boon companions of yore aren't young enough any more to enjoy night life. They have calmed down like me. If I am in a country where the television is on during the late hours I watch television after I get back to my hotel. If not I go to bed immediately to be able to rise early next morning. Generally, I am up at eight o'clock. If I am in an unknown town I rise even earlier, and go out to study the town and its people. I take my camera with me. I walk a great deal, I don't visit too many museums—I am not a museum fan—and in any case most museums show you more or less similar objects. What I enjoy watching most is the daily life of the natives of the town.

In some countries I explore more than in others. In Italy I am always on my feet because the Italians are born actors. They can be vehement, they cry, they shout, they fight—no, not really though they give you the impression they are ready to kill each other. Truly I love exploring Italian streets.

There are also countries where I have friends, in the

United States for instance. In America I have less time to roam the streets because I spend most of it with my friends, and we talk and talk till the cows come home. The art of conversation is dead, but there are some survivors left, and I consider myself as one of them.

Chapter Fifteen

In 1972 I moved with Ulla and our children to the French part of Switzerland.

In France the profession of the artiste is considered a luxury. The official outlook is that listening to chansons is like drinking champagne or buying expensive scent. No French government has perceived yet that the French chanson and those who sing it abroad are an excellent means of publicity for France. The Americans, on the other hand, have fully realised the importance of jazz and American music as part and parcel of American life, and have helped their singers and musicians to propagate American culture in foreign countries. Take Brazil. When the Brazilian government wanted their music and singers to be known outside the country, they put up a lot of money to achieve that. Nothing of the sort has ever been done in France. Because our profession is considered as an item of luxury we the chansonniers aren't allowed any expenses when we pay our income tax. A manufacturer is of course. He can claim expense allowances even when he hasn't any expenses.

I was getting fed up with that state of affairs. If I go on tour in France, say one that lasts for a year, I cover in my car more than a hundred thousand kilometres. It isn't necessary to point out that after a hundred thousand kilometres a car isn't worth much any more, yet one gets no income tax rebate for the new car one is compelled to buy. The same goes for one's stage suits, linen, and everything else one has to buy to be able to pursue one's professional career. When I realised that I wasn't only paying exorbitant tax but tax on the tax I had already paid I decided to move to Switzerland with my family, and become residents there. I had naively imagined that the French authorities would have second thoughts when they heard of my departure, and do something for our profession, that is give us a new status. Alas, nothing of the sort happened. We continue to be considered as luxury goods.

Despite all the grand talk about the arts in France artists and artistes are looked upon as negligible people. No film star, however great and famous, has as large photographs on hoardings as any unknown candidate at an election. The candidates can deduct those photographs as expenses, whereas we wouldn't be allowed to. I can't see why politicians should be more entitled to star treatment than us.

When I went to live in Switzerland with my wife and children the French authorities searched for ways and means to force me back to France. They decided that by moving to Switzerland I had infringed the French exchange regulations. In short, they refused to accept the fact that I had become a resident in a foreign country. After six years of residing in Switzerland they still consider me a resident of France. Thus every time I earn money in foreign countries and that money is transferred to my bank account in Switzerland they give me a fresh fine, and those fines mount up. It is useless to argue with them. All I earn in France with my singing and my records is held back to pay the fines.

Switzerland is considered a fiscal paradise, but that isn't quite so. One pays heavy taxes, but they are just taxes. An artiste's general expenses are deducted from his income tax, and that in my case is important indeed. People ask why has Aznavour chosen to live in Switzerland? When they ask that they give the question a sort of nasty meaning as if Switzerland stood for secret vices and strange habits. If somebody chooses to live in Belgium or Canada and is a Frenchman nobody thinks there could be anything wrong about that. They seem to forget that in French Switzerland, French is the native language the same way as in France or Canada or the Walloon part of Belgium. So I am no expatriate. In fact, I live in a French speaking world in the same fashion as I had lived in France. I insist on that point since I am more French by language than by blood.

As I am approaching the end of this book I can't help thinking of all the catastrophes that dropped like bricks on my head during my long struggles, and made it impossible for me to acquire a fortune however modest. Yet fortune was often within my reach. An artiste like me is frequently surrounded by unscrupulous people, and if they are likeable too then woe to the poor artiste. I trusted many people in the course of my career, and it usually took me a long time to discover they were harming me financially. I let them look after my financial interests since I am no business man: they looked only after their own financial interests. Of course, I deserve blame too, for I like spending money, and at times I spent more than I earned. My fundamental bad luck was that I didn't find any one to say to me—You have so much to spend, and the rest you will put aside.

I confess I never managed to put money aside. Anyhow, big fortunes aren't made by singers. I know the uninitiated believe we make fortunes. But let us look at facts. A theatre with two thousand seats remains a theatre with two thousand seats, and the price of the seats is arranged before the performance. Even if the sum the artiste earns is considerable he has to deduct general expenses and taxes. If one hasn't the strength or foresight to invest the sums one earns they will disappear, leaving no trace behind.

Financial worries and losses I had from the start. My parents had to sell their furniture to enable me to go on tour, then I lost the suitcase that contained all I possessed. Bad luck continued to rain down on me, and when at long last I was beginning to earn good money and acquire fame there came my car accident with eighteen months of unemployment in the wake of it. When I went on tour with my own company it was a total failure yet I continued paying the company because it wasn't their fault that I didn't draw audiences. I travelled to countries that weren't interested in the chanson, and I lost heavily. The point I wish to make is that I always had to start afresh.

France is the perfect example. All I possessed there has been seized by the authorities, the exchange regulations their unbelievable excuse. The more my records earn in France the larger will be the fines. Nonetheless, I don't complain. I don't know how to look after and keep money, but I do know how to run my private life.

As I have said before I work hard while I am on tour so as to be free when I get back to my wife and children. I live according to their timetable when I am at home. Ulla and I have three children, Patricia, my eldest, lives in Hollywood. She has a small daughter, thus I am a grandfather in America.

We get up early in the morning because the children are already awake. My wife prepares the breakfast while I go to the baker to buy fresh bread. I do that every morning, and I find that very important. We have no servants because I believe that servants stand in the way of close family life. If the servants look after the children, the children become strangers to their parents. Patricia and I were very close during her childhood. I want the same relations with my three small children.

My wife's and my great luxury is having separate bathrooms. Not to fall over one another when one gets up is my idea of peace and luxury. After breakfast—the children are at school—we go shopping together, although I often go shopping alone. My wife deserves that consideration since she has to do all the shopping on her own while I am away singing.

We live beside Lake Geneva, and I frequently wander down to the small port. I know everybody in our village, and when I stroll around I stop in the little inns to drink a glass of wine with the local folk. Then I walk back to the house, where there is always some work waiting for me, a piece of furniture to repair or a drawer that has fallen out in my absence to attend to. Then I look at my mail, read all the letters, then file them. I have a secretary who comes in every five days to type answers to letters that don't interest me. I answer personal letters myself.

In the afternoon I fetch the children from school, and I devote myself to them till they go to bed. My little daughter is nine years old, my sons are seven and fifteen months old. In the evenings my wife and I either look at television or go to the theatre or the cinema. If we stay in we go to bed at half past nine.

I don't think that the years change a person's outlook overmuch. It widens but remains fundamentally the same. In many ways memories make the man. When I was a little boy I saw my mother bending over the sewing machine for long hours. When Ulla and I moved into our house in Switzerland the first thing I bought was a sewing machine. My wife couldn't help asking me, 'Why do you insist on a sewing machine? Nobody sews in this house.'

'Because a sewing machine means a great deal to me,' I replied.

I smiled as I said that. If I am asked whether I consider myself an Armenian immigrant I look at the sewing machine and say, 'Yes.'

Of course the public is less interested in Charles Aznavour the family man than in the Charles Aznavour they see on the stage. I believe I have chiefly conquered my public in so many different countries with my understanding of their worries and troubles. They say to themselves, Look, it hasn't happened only to me, and feel better. I have also an instinctive knowledge of what goes on in their minds, and are unable to express in words. That is why I am often told, 'Isn't it strange that you say exactly what I feel?' Or, 'You tell in your song something that has happened to me too.' I am in a way a chronicler of our age, sentiments and feelings. The public knows that.

Male spectators expect me to say not too kind things about women, and are pleased when they hear me saying them.

Women spectators expect the contrary, and I oblige them too. They enjoy it when I sing of men of fifty who strut about in jeans, and consider themselves still young. I only say the truth in my songs, and that is what the public appreciates. And I have a language of my own. When I want to say *merde* I say it; when I want to say piss I say piss; and when I feel like saying my arse I don't hesitate to say my arse.

The Anglo-Saxons have a Puritan foundation. I am thinking of their songs, not of their vocabulary. 'Bloody' and 'fucking' I hear all over the place when I am in an Anglo-Saxon country. My vocabulary is the same in my chansons as in my speech. As I get older my language becomes franker, and people flock to hear it. I am no goody-goody on the boards. My movements and gestures are all my own too, and I simply couldn't change them.

The orchestra never plays when I appear on the stage because I couldn't assert myself in all that noise. I must create my own climate, and to achieve that the audience must be conscious only of my appearance on the stage. If the orchestra makes a lot of noise when the artiste makes his entry the public gets quite the wrong impression of him. Some artistes believe that with a noisy orchestra the applause will be noisier—a very wrong idea.

Thoughout my entire career I have believed in personal freedom. The star system is the enemy of freedom. Being a star is the same thing as being a slave. The star has to keep his distance from the rest of mankind, must live in an ivory tower, and must spread mystery round himself. I care neither for legend nor mystery. I want to live as it suits me and come and go as I like. I enjoy chatting with people, and thanks to that I learn languages and understand what the people feel. The talk of ordinary people is the basis of my inspiration. I firmly believe that a creative artist must be and remain in close touch with the world he lives and moves in. The gentleman who retires to his study is unable to understand the language of ordinary people which is the language of the heart. I always choose the language of the heart, and I frankly prefer it to the language of the brain.

My profession suits me perfectly as it is a profession for tramps and vagabonds.

When I go on tour I engage musicians but never other artistes. I consider my public performances as concerts, and I am sure they are concerts. The French chansons as practised by Trenet, Brassens and Brel are nearer to concerts than an ordinary repertoire of songs. When the Anglo-Saxons come on the stage they don't only sing but chat with the spectators and tell jokes. Our approach is entirely different because the idea of the French chanson is nearer to the concert hall than the music hall. I am the Menuhin of the chanson, and what is more I am like a father who has children singing successfully all over the world because of my influence on modern ballads.

I want to end this book evoking my mother to whom I owe so much. Although my father, who died in 1978 at a great age, played a more active part in my life these last pages are for my mother. She was the pivot of the family. She had admitted from the day of her marriage that my father was a marvellous madman and she treated him accordingly till the end of her life. Father drank heavily, chased women, but he was always back home when we needed him. Mother taught me how to treat the fair sex and how to look at women when I was merely a child. I laugh when I hear high falutin' talk about women's lib. In our household the women, whether mother or sister, had their complete freedom. And the women with whom I have lived can thank mother for my easy relationship with them. With me there always was total equality between men and women.

My sister's and my gifts were developed by mother. She'd had a better education than father, and she would probably have gone much further in her stage career if the Turks hadn't massacred her parents. But what she had and what she knew she handed down to us. We heard father sing, but mother talked of music and poetry and people and how to treat them. Mother wasn't a singer:

she was an actress, yet she sang to us when we were small, and thus music and song seeped into us.

When my sister and I decided to go on the stage it wasn't Father who agreed to it or encouraged us. 'The mother brings up the children,' he said, 'so it is for the mother to decide.' It was mother who agreed and encouraged us, and taught us many things about the stage which with our lack of means we couldn't have learnt from anybody else. Forty-five years ago one still had to pay for any sort of schooling.

Mother was an excellent needlewoman and dressmaker, and she worked day and night. My sister and I were treated as equals by her. There was no question of boys do this and girls do that. Boy and girl had exactly the same responsibilities. Yes, I can thank mother for my outlook and approach to life.

When at the age of nine I went on tour for the first time mother accompanied me to the station. We were several children in that troupe, and Metz was our destination. In Metz I went into the station restaurant with another little boy and we took an expensive meal with our earnings which, needless to say, weren't large sums, fifty francs in all.

On my return mother asked, 'What did you do in Metz after the performance?'

'I went to a restaurant, where I had rabbit. It cost twenty-two francs.'

Twenty-two francs was a fortune for us poor Armenians, yet mother was pleased because her son had enjoyed his meal.

Index